KU-766-550

Contents

Introduction

Welcome to the *10 Minute Guide to Time Management*. This slim volume will provide you with the essence of what you need to effectively manage your time. You'll learn how to set goals and to identify priorities, differentiate between the urgent and the important, be better organized, handle mail and correspondence, master basic technologies, keep interruptions to a minimum, and gain more time through effective delegation. You will also learn how to limit the effects of procrastination, say no with confidence, keep stress at acceptable levels, conduct more streamlined meetings, be more effective in using your time on the road, and, in general, keep your life in balance.

Here's what you won't encounter: long lists of things you have to do, complicated procedures, and steadfast rules that don't apply to the ever-changing situations that you face. Instead, you will learn simple but effective techniques for staying in control of your time. The common denominator to these techniques is that you can apply them to all the various situations in which you find yourself.

The 10 Minute Guide series is structured so that you can complete each lesson in about 10 minutes. Hence, the whole program would take no more than three hours if you proceeded from Lesson 1 straight through to Lesson 14. A better approach might be to tackle one lesson per day. So in less than three weeks, you can learn and apply everything in this guide.

ACKNOWLEDGMENTS

Marie Butler-Knight first suggested that I take on the project. Susan M. Davidson, with help from Elizabeth Yurkes, transcribed the entire manuscript. Renee Wilmeth at Macmillan offered insightful editorial guidance. Valerie Davidson, age 9, let Daddy work undisturbed so that he could finish the project by the due date.

LESSON 1

Understanding Time Management

In this lesson, you will learn the nature of time, explore the common myths surrounding time management, and develop a strategy that will allow you to systematically increase your personal productivity.

GRASP THE NATURE OF TIME

You know that there are 24 hours in a day and 168 hours in a week. You also know that sometimes these periods of time seem to race by without warning, offering you far less than the actual number of hours.

You don't have to study theoretical physics to understand that for all practical purposes, time is relative. When you're facing a deadline, the minutes seem to click off the clock at a faster pace than when you're attending a lecture that bores you senseless. In the daily rush of contemporary society, too many hours seem to go by in far less than sixty minutes. When you get to spend an hour with a long lost friend or someone you genuinely look forward to seeing, for example, it seems as if you cover so much ground within that hour; compare this to how quickly an hour passes when you watch two television sitcoms.

CAUTION

The more tasks and activities you attempt to cram into a fixed time period, the faster that time period seems to go by—and the less you're likely to enjoy the time at all.

Why do we feel uncomfortable when our time races along? Human physiology has been in formation for tens of thousands of years; it took us a long time to develop into the type of species that we are today. Meanwhile, contemporary society is moving faster and faster. At work, more phone calls, more faxes, more e-mail, and more people knocking at our office doors all but ensure that each hour races by, at least from a perceptual standpoint. At home, more TV stations, more movies, more magazines, more books, and a greater variety of consumer goods all conspire to make it seem as if each hour and each day is flying by.

LESS CAN BE MORE ENJOYABLE

All around us society says, "Take on more; click me; sign on." However, we can only cram so much into a week, a day, or an hour. And we can only focus on so much. These days, it's rare to encounter advice that says

- Take on less.
- Limit the field.
- Be more selective.

TIP

To maintain control of your time, it's wise not to have too many things competing for your time and attention.

Although there may be exponential growth in the number of items that compete for our time and attention, our lives are quite finite. You will die, I will die, everyone will die. Hopefully, each of us will die after a long and happy life. When we get to the end of our lives, will we be able to look back and say that we had time for reflection, time for quiet moments, and long stretches when things did not race by?

RIGHT NOW IS EVERYTHING

One of the keys to effective use of time involves recognizing a fundamental principle put forth by Robert Fritz, author of *The Path of Least Resistance*. He writes, "Right now is the most important moment in your life." How does Fritz know that right now, this moment, is the most important moment in each of our lives? What does he mean by this bold statement? Fritz is saying that at any given moment in your life, particularly right now, you should recognize that you can only take action in the present. For example, you can only enjoy your meal right now, or your workout, or that challenging assignment you're tackling.

TIP

If you know that right now is the most important moment, and then the next moment is the most important moment, and then the next and so on, you are far more inclined to be judicious with the use of your time.

Picture this: You're supposed to work on a project, but instead you're dawdling, or engaged in trivia, or diverting your attention in five other directions. Are you truly acknowledging that right now is the most important moment in your life? Probably not. When you can acknowledge that right now is the most important time of your life, it is far easier for you to concentrate on the task at hand. Plan to do this hour's job this hour, this day's work today, and so on.

More than a hundred years ago, Bruce Barton wrote, "The most important thing about getting somewhere is starting right where we are. "Less than a score later, Theodore Roosevelt said, "Do what you can, with what you have, where you are."

How can you ever get some place if you don't start with where you are?

Right now, you're starting by reading Lesson 1 of this book, and delving into the nature of time. Good for you. It's worth your while, so stay with it. Don't turn on the TV; don't have music playing in the background; don't run to the refrigerator. Instead, stay right here and recognize that right now is the most important moment in your life.

CUT THROUGH THE MYTHS SURROUNDING TIME MANAGEMENT

Managing your time is a worthwhile pursuit; beware, though—the myths surrounding the effective management of time can all but quash your efforts.

Time management, as we know it, essentially started with the work of Frederick Taylor and Frank Gilbreth.

PLAIN ENGLISH

Time and motion studies   The attempt to elicit greater productivity from workers by closely examining their workstations, movements, and available resources.

One hundred years ago, they astounded the industrial world by establishing time and motion procedures that enabled employers to get higher productivity from their workers. In doing so, Taylor and Gilbreth established the basis of modern day time management techniques, which were widely adopted by executives.

In recent years, the backlash against Taylor, in particular, has been mighty. Some authors contend that his ceaseless quest for "the one best way" changed the very texture of twentieth-century life. Others contend that Taylor taught us *not* to stop and smell the roses, and that his compulsions eerily foreshadowed that time-pressure that everyone feels today.

CAUTION

> More information is generated on Earth every hour than you could partake of in the rest of your life.

In any case, the industrial age has given over to the dawn of the information age. As I see it, the current difficulty is that we all face too much information, and that today many myths still abound as to what constitutes effective time management. Time management is subjective, varying from one situation to another. For example, time management advocates often advise handling each piece of paper that comes across your desk once. This sounds like reasonable advice; however, the number of times you handle a piece of paper should always depend on the contents or significance of the piece of paper.

Some pieces of paper are worth handling twenty-five times or more. Most pieces of paper, though, are best handled zero times—in short, never. You'll want to set up systems where much of what used to come across your desk never even comes into your field of vision. I will discuss this more in subsequent lessons.

CAUTION

> Every time you're exposed to paper, articles, or documents that are not related to what you are working on in your career or your life, you potentially add to the glut of all the things that compete for your time and attention, and perceptually make the hours slide by faster.

THE LIMITS ALL AROUND US

Suppose I start stacking bricks on a table, and that I can go as high as I want. What will eventually happen? The table will fall over—there are structural limits as to how much weight the table can bear. Or, suppose I start stuffing college students into a Volkswagen Beetle. How many will fit? Who knows? If they are all slender, more will fit than if they are not. Whether it's six, eight, or ten students, at some point, I can't get another student into the car—there are spatial limitations.

Bearing this in mind, why, in allowing all manner of paper to cross our desks and all other things to compete for our time and attention, do we pretend that we can take on more and more and more, not paying attention to the temporal (time) limits that each of us face? An hour will remain 60 minutes, a week will remain 168 hours and so forth.

 TIP

> The myth of "handling each piece of paper once" must give way to the reality that most pieces of paper should never cross your desk at all.

WHEN SPEED IS NOT DESIRABLE

Another myth of time management is that of the need to complete things faster. You see ads in magazines for speed-reading, speed listening, speed learning, and so on. The anthropological reality, however, is that we walk, talk, eat, and read—as well as listen and learn—at a certain pace for a reason.

When you attempt to undertake any bodily function, such as eating or talking, at a speed that is faster than is comfortable for you, you actually do harm to yourself. In the short run, you can get by with this kind of behavior. In the long run, though, you'll be prone to stress, anxiety, ulcers, and reduced immunity.

 TIP

> You need to operate at a pace that is comfortable for you.

If you feel time pressured because of the responsibilities and tasks facing you, you must learn to marshal the resources necessary to meet the challenge (which I'll discuss in subsequent lessons). However, don't walk faster, talk faster, eat faster, and sleep less in the attempt to be more productive.

PLANNING AND SCHEDULING TOOLS ARE NOT OMNISCIENT

Another time management myth, particularly common in recent years, is that you must rely on sophisticated scheduling tools as if they are the be all and end all. It only makes sense to use palm top organizers, electronic calendars, time management software, day planners, and so on if they …

- Support the way you live and work.

- Are convenient and easy for you to use.

- Are always up-to-date.

> **PLAIN ENGLISH**
>
> **Scheduling tools**   Palmtop organizers, electronic calendars, time management software, day planners and any other device that supports one's use of time and productivity.

> **CAUTION**
>
> I bet you can't name a time management tool in the entire world that won't let you down the minute you cease to maintain it.

Even with forthcoming voice recognition time management scheduling tools, you will still have to "feed" the system. I will cover how to select and use a planner effectively in Lesson 4, "Scheduling for Results." For now, recognize that all tools you use to schedule your time—from simple to-do lists to complicated scheduling software—require your continual input and updating; otherwise, they quickly fail to reflect your current reality—including the tasks and responsibilities you face.

Moreover, until sophisticated time management tools come packed with a mechanical arm that literally moves the items that have been placed on your desk, logs them in, and then ranks them based on the workload you already face, you will forever be out of sync.

CAUTION

> Until time management tools check your e-mail, fax machine, or voice mail, and similarly assess and rank what each of those messages represents in terms of what you now have to accomplish, you will continue to be out of sync.

Put simply, your brain is the most important tool in managing your schedule, your time, and your life.

WORK SMARTER ACCORDING TO WHOM?

Another time management myth involves the notion that you must work smarter, not harder. If you had perfect information, a team of advisors, and an abundance of relevant resources, I suppose you'd have the opportunity to work smarter rather than harder. But what does "work smarter" really mean? Was Thomas Edison smarter after making more than 8,000 attempts to identify the proper filament in making the light bulb? After he finally found the right filament, did his IQ suddenly rise?

Working longer and being open to new ideas can help you to work smarter. To simply say to someone, "Work smarter, not harder," is out of context. Keep in mind that "work smarter, not harder" really means that you should take a little time to think about what you want to accomplish so that you start off in the right direction and assemble the necessary resources. This, in turn, increases the odds that you'll be able to complete the job more quickly and easily.

TIP

> Sometimes the only way to work smarter is to work hard so that the insights that enable you to work smarter finally emerge!

INCREASE YOUR PERSONAL PRODUCTIVITY

Drawing upon Robert Fritz's observation that "right now is the most important moment of your life," you will find that you have the opportunity to systematically increase your personal productivity at any moment of the day. Similarly, Alan Lakein, author of *How to Get Control of Your Time and Your Life*, advised his readers to constantly ask themselves the following question: "What's the highest and best use of my time?" Fritz's observation, coupled with Lakein's question, produces a powerful combination.

On the one hand, you acknowledge that this moment is the most important moment of your life—the only moment when you can take action. At the same time, you ask yourself, "What would be the highest and best use of my time at this important moment?"

When you ask yourself this question, strange and wonderful answers often emerge:

- Sometimes the highest and best use of your time is to simply take a walk. For example, this is true when you're facing a tough problem and are not thinking clearly. A walk can help to clear out your mind. Sometimes, when you come back, the correct path simply emerges.

- Sometimes the highest and best use of your time is to look out the window and reflect; to make a key telephone call; or to lock your door, turn off the ringer on your phone, and barricade yourself in until you finish a particular task.

The highest and best use of your time often involves marshaling the resources you need to complete the project or task on time and within budget. Too many career professionals today throw their time and life at a problem, deplete their physical resources, and incur all kinds of stress and anxiety. They might finish by the deadline, but at what cost personally?

> **CAUTION**
> It's okay occasionally to maintain a deadline orientation. You will get things done; there is no real harm if you do this now and again. But if a deadline mentality ensues, meaning that's the way you do things all the time, you're either going to shorten your life or diminish your quality of life.

Determining the highest and best use of your time may necessitate clearing your desk, assembling material you need to tackle the project at hand, and delving into it headlong. Furthermore, determining the highest and best use of your time in the most important moment of your life, which is always the present moment, may require that you ask your boss for additional resources in the form of staff help, technology, or lesser burden in other areas.

RELY ON YOUR INNER WISDOM

You already have a strong idea as to how to best proceed with most any situation that you face—even highly challenging situations. Too often, the problem is that you don't follow your own inner wisdom. Instead, you let yourself be buffed by external sources that in reality offer little contribution.

Rely on your instincts more often. Recent discoveries have demonstrated that there is far more to instinct, intuition, and gut feelings than was previously imagined. All the cellular intelligence throughout your body is called upon when you make a decision based on instinct. It is not random, it is not whimsical, and it is not foolish. Decisions based on instinct and intuition rapidly and automatically encompass all your life experiences and acquired knowledge.

THE 30-SECOND RECAP

- Recognize that the more items there are competing for your time and attention, the more time seems to speed by. Your quest should be to have fewer stimuli, to increase your powers of concentration on the task at hand, and to maintain your focus.

- Right now is the most important moment in your life, as is the next, and then the next. The realization that here and now is the only place in which you can take action is simple yet profound.

- Walk, talk, eat, read, and live in a manner that is comfortable for you. Don't fall prey to the false economy of speeding up bodily functions in the hope that this will somehow make you more efficient in the long run. Marshall the resources you need to handle a task, instead of continually throwing your time and life at tasks.

- Keep asking yourself the following question: "What is the highest and best use of my time right now?"

- Trust your instincts; they represent your accumulated experiences and acquired knowledge.

Lesson 2
Shaping Your Future

In this lesson, you will learn how to identify priorities, set goals, and achieve the important things in life, in spite of the many demands on your time.

The Importance of Establishing Priorities

Why should you bother establishing priorities? When you identify what's important in your life, you are in a better position to meet the challenges and demands you face on a daily basis that can otherwise fritter away your time.

PLAIN ENGLISH

Your life's priorities   That which is most important to you.

Some people say that seeing their good friends on a regular basis is important, yet they make the cross-town trip only once a month. Some people say that maintaining their health and level of fitness is important, yet they never seem to find the time to exercise. Establishing and paying homage to the choices in your life that are important to you and how you prefer to dispense your time in pursuit of those priorities is essential to your having a more fulfilling life and managing your time more effectively.

The Broad Categories of Life

Your life's priorities are uniquely yours. However, most people's priorities fall into a few basic categories. To help you get started with creating a list of priorities, take a look at the seven broad categories identified by Dr. Tony Alessandra:

1. **Mental:** Mental priorities might include improving your intellect, improving your memory, increasing your concentration, being a better learner, and being more creative.

2. **Physical:** Physical priorities could include achieving and maintaining overall fitness; acquiring skills in particular sports; improving agility, stamina, and endurance; and having a good level of well-being.

3. **Family:** Priorities related to family might include having a better relationship with your spouse, children, parents, siblings, or other loved ones. This category also encompasses the special people you consider to be part of your extended family.

4. **Social:** Social priorities might include being part of your community and having relationships with people in your neighborhood and outside of the family, as well as relationships with people in your business and industry. In short, priorities in this category ensure that your friends have an important part in your life.

5. **Spiritual:** Spiritual priorities might include having religion play a large part in your life, strengthening your relationship between you and your creator, becoming a humanitarian, and developing a personal philosophy.

6. **Career:** Career priorities might include rising to a certain level in your profession, gaining recognition, and achieving particular milestones. Priorities in this category can also encompass having a positive influence on others or developing yourself in unique ways.

7. **Financial:** Financial priorities could include securing your nest egg, putting your children through college, buying that dream house, and otherwise establishing a financial safety net for you and your loved ones.

This list is general; you may have major priority areas that aren't listed here. Perhaps one or more of the categories on the previous list aren't priority areas for you at all. The key notion is that you need to identify your priorities so that you can establish goals that will support those priorities. I can't give you an exact number, but you want to have only a few priorities in life. Eighteen is probably too much, and three might be too few. The number varies from person to person. In general, though, you should have just a handful of priorities. After all, a priority is a part of your life that you have identified as important. If you have too many priorities, then, paradoxically, they can't all be priorities!

CAUTION

If you have too many priorities, you are not likely to give each the required respect.

THE NITTY-GRITTY OF IDENTIFYING PRIORITIES

The procedure that follows is simple and direct and will help you establish priorities. Be careful! Priorities are broad elements of life. They are so basic that you can often misplace them somewhere in your go-go schedule. To stay on top of your priorities, follow these steps:

1. Write down everything that is important to you or that you seek to achieve. Feel free to make this list long and involved.

2. Revisit your list several hours later or even the next day. Cross out everything that, on second reading, no longer appears crucial. Combine any items that appear similar to each other. Your goal is to dramatically pare down your list.

CAUTION

> If you have too many priorities, you are likely to feel anxious and frustrated, which is how most people these days feel most of the time.

3. Restructure, redefine, and rewrite your list if necessary. Keep looking to streamline it. If you are not sure if an item belongs on the list, the chances are that it does not.

4. Put your list away and take it out the next day or the day after that. Now review it as if you are seeing it for the first time. Can any items be combined? Can anything be dropped? Should anything be reworded? As always, if something seems as if it is not that important, it probably isn't, so feel free to drop it. Go ahead and create a working list of what you feel are your priorities at this time. Yes, things will shift and change as time marches on. After all, your priorities are based on what you identify as important in your life at a particular point in time, and because the details of your life are constantly changing, it makes sense that your priorities will change as well.

For now, however, concentrate on the few key important areas in your life and make them part of your list. For each of the items on your list, consider using an active, positive verb phrase, as in the following examples:

- "Achieve financial independence"

- "Strengthen my relationship with my spouse"

- "Provide for the education of my children"

By wording your priorities in this way, you are more inclined to take action than if you simply say "happy marriage" or "children's education."

You might find it particularly helpful if you print your priorities on a small card that you can keep in your scheduler, purse, appointment book, or wallet. Carrying your list with you affords you the opportunity to review your priorities periodically throughout the day, particularly when you are stuck in a line somewhere. Losing sight of the things we have deemed as important is all too easy in our rush-rush world. Simply reading your list of priorities on a regular basis is powerful and reinforcing. As Dr. Tony Alessandra put it, reading your priority list often contributes to "your sensation of owning your life."

PLAIN ENGLISH

> **Priority list**   A simple roster, preferably easy to access, that names a handful of things in life important to you.

GOALS TO SUPPORT YOUR PRIORITIES

You can establish a variety of goals in support of each of the priority areas you have chosen. Suppose that health and fitness are a priority for you; you can establish several goals to support this priority. For example, your stated goal could be: "I will join a health club this week and visit the gym at least three times a week for a 45-minute workout."

TIP

It is essential when establishing a goal to be as precise as possible.

Notice that this goal is very specific; it provides precise timelines and numbers. If you were to simply say, "I'll join a health club and work out a lot," you're not likely to get the same results as using a more precise statement. When will you join the health club? How often will you go? How long will you work out? Numbers and specific timelines give you something to strive for. Visiting the gym at least three times a week for a 45-minute workout is much different than simply being in the health club, gabbing with someone else, heading over to the juice machine, leaving early, and pretending that you got a good workout. By contrast, if rising in your career is one of your priorities, you might want to add these specific goals to your list:

• To achieve a salary of $__,000 by December 31 of this year.

• To finish the three courses at the local community college this semester, so I'll have the requisite skills to move into *x* position.

• To add two more people to my staff by the end of the month so that I will have the opportunity in the next quarter to experience supervising a staff of six.

• To be transferred to the London office for two years by the end of the next quarter.

When setting your goals, follow these guidelines:

1. **Be sure the goal you set is something that you want to do as opposed to something that you have to do.** As I discuss in the *Complete Idiot's Guide to Reaching Your Goals*, your goals do not initially have to be set by you. If you are in sales, your sales manager may set your monthly or quarterly sales quota. Yet you can make a goal your own even if it is

initially imposed upon you. There could be many very good reasons why you personally want to achieve that goal, such as an increase in income, competitive spirit, pride, or a job promotion.

2. **Establish your goals in positive terms, using positive terminology.** If one of your priority areas is health and fitness, and you have been chain smoking for 10 years, it won't help to set a goal such as, "I will not smoke for one week." What happens during that week? You begin to dwell on smoking day after day, hour after hour, until you get to the point where you can barely stand it. A more effective goal statement would be "I will maintain clear, clean lungs this week."

3. **Write down your goals.** Writing down your goals helps solidify your efforts. Having your goals in a place where you can review them makes them more real. At the least, written goals serve as a visual reminder and confirmation of their importance. At the most, they are the guiding formula that will lead to a highly desirable end result.

PLAIN ENGLISH

Reinforcement   Reward directly following a particular behavior.

WAYS TO REINFORCE YOUR GOALS

Anybody can establish goals. Unfortunately, most people's goals are all but forgotten days or weeks after they first establish them. Reinforcing the goals that you set so that you will achieve them is much tougher. Fortunately, there are many techniques you can employ to see that you stick to the goals that you set for yourself. For example, you could try the following:

- Join a group of like-minded individuals

- Harness the power of deadlines

- Visualize the completion of your goals

- Create back-up systems

Let's look at these options in more detail. Joining up with those who have common goals with you is a time-honored tradition in accomplishing goals. This might involve joining an organized group of people who have common goals (for example, many people who want to stay sober have joined Alcoholics Anonymous) or simply finding a friend who wants to achieve the same thing you do at around the same time you do.

Being accountable and reporting your progress to one or more others helps to ensure that your progress will continue. For example, if you tell me that you are going to accomplish something by next week, then next week when we meet, I will ask you about your goal. You'll either tell me that you accomplished it, or you will tell me something different. Simply knowing that we will be meeting and discussing the accomplishment of your goal may be the driving force that you need to be successful in achieving it.

 TIP

> When you have no one to report to, it is easy to slide. Having someone who is waiting to hear about your progress will increase the odds of your success.

Harnessing the power of deadlines also works well for many people. Up to now, you may have dreaded deadlines, seeing them as something imposed upon you that routinely fosters stress and anxiety. Yet deadlines can serve as powerful motivators toward the accomplishment of your goals.

For example, my contract for this book stated that I would turn in a certain portion of my manuscript by a certain date. If I had tried to write the entire book at once, I would have never finished it. Instead, my goal in approaching this book was to write one chapter at a time.

In fact, because the chapters are made of subsections, I simply aimed to finish one subsection at a time, until I had finished a chapter. By the time I was finished with a chapter, I felt so good about my work for that day that the rest of the day seemed like a vacation.

The next day, I went back and started another chapter, approaching it one subsection at a time and always keeping the deadlines in mind. Without a contract that clearly stated the milestone dates by which I had to deliver portions of my manuscript, the likelihood of my delivering the work on time (if at all) would have dramatically decreased.

 TIP

Always consider what deadlines you face that you can turn around and use to your advantage. What deadlines can you impose upon yourself to increase the probability of you achieving your goals?

Visualizing the completion of your goals is another powerful technique for increasing your probability of success. Most sports heroes today visualize successfully completing the foul shot, catching the touchdown pass, hitting the home run, completing the triple axle jump, or clearing the hurdle before engaging in the sport. By visualizing their performance, these pros increase their odds of success. Likewise, virtuoso pianists, ballet dancers, and even professional speakers visualize successfully engaging in the task at hand before they perform.

 TIP

Visualizing yourself successfully completing the steps that lead to a goal you have established will increase your chances of success.

You probably visualize all the time by thinking about being with a loved one, having dinner that evening, or skiing during your next vacation in Colorado. You can use the same process to see yourself completing your goals.

Any goal, large or small, lends itself to the visualization process. Find a quiet place where you won't be disturbed, close your eyes, and let your imagination take hold. See yourself accomplishing exactly what you want to accomplish, in the way you want to accomplish it. If your goal is to achieve your ideal weight, visualize yourself working out and enjoying it and then stepping on the scale and seeing the pounds go down. Visualize yourself in front of the mirror without your love handles or without saddlebag thighs. See yourself as the trimmed, toned you that you know you can be.

PLAIN ENGLISH

Backup system   An established procedure whereby you help to reinforce established goals.

Creating back-up systems is another powerful technique that can help you reinforce your goals. Surround yourself with goal reminders; use Post-It notes that list your goal-reinforcing statements and post them on a mirror, in your appointment book, on the dashboard of your car, on or near your nightstand, on the refrigerator, by your front door, and wherever you are likely to pass during the course of a day.

Write something that is uplifting and supportive of your efforts such as, "Today is going to be a great day for accomplishing my goals of ...." Vary the statements so that you don't start to ignore them. Put them in creative places where you know you will encounter them and where they will have the most impact.

I like to leave a note to myself in my appointment book at the end of each day. When I open up the appointment book to start the upcoming day, I see the uplifting note, smile broadly, and get to work.

THE 30-SECOND RECAP

- Priorities are the most important things in your life, so you can only have so many of them. If you have too many priorities, then, paradoxically, they can't all be priorities.

- For many people, priorities fall into seven broad categories including mental, physical, family, social, career, and financial priorities.

- Establishing written, specific goals with timelines is an effective way to support your priorities. Using a variety of goal-reinforcing techniques increases the probability that you will accomplish the goal.

LESSON 3

Avoiding the Tyranny of the Urgent

In this lesson, you will learn to differentiate between the urgent and the important and be able to use the Pareto Principle to identify your areas of focus.

KNOW WHAT'S IMPORTANT

If I could construct a simple grid into which all items that compete for your time and attention might fall, it would look like this:

	Urgent	Not Urgent
Important	1	2
Not important	3	4

Quadrant 1 holds those items that are important and urgent. Quadrant 2 collects those items that are important and not urgent. Quadrant 3 has those items that are not important but urgent, and Quadrant 4 holds those items that are not important and not urgent.

All too often in the workaday world, we find ourselves engaging in tasks that are urgent but, in retrospect, not important. If you could manage your time in an ideal way, then as often as possible you would focus on those tasks that are important and urgent. Assuming that urgency announces itself, like the rent coming due, the real question is knowing what's important.

In his lectures, author Dr. Stephen Covey contends that if you do pay homage to the most important things in your life, as you've identified them, you begin to find ways to fit everything. He uses the analogy of filling a glass jar with rocks, pebbles, and sand. If you begin to fill the jar with the pebbles and sand, you run the risk of not being able to get all the rocks into the jar. Now suppose you put the rocks in first, followed by some of the smaller pebbles, and then sprinkle in the sand. Voilà! Everything fits into the jar.

PLAIN ENGLISH

Urgent   That which cries out for attention independent of its importance, typically announcing itself much like a microwave beeping when it's time to take the food out of it.

In this analogy, the rocks represent important tasks that support your priority. The pebbles represent secondary tasks that are perhaps urgent but not important, and the grains of sand represent tasks that are neither important nor urgent. When you deal with the rocks first, a magical thing happens: You still find room for the secondary and tertiary items. They fit in and around the spaces available. If you attempt to do it the other way around, too often you end up giving short shrift to what is truly important in your life and dissipating your energy and efforts on the minutiae of life.

TIP

Stop doing what's unimportant and without urgency. Where the important and the urgent intersect (Quadrant 1) is where you need to expend most of your energies.

APPLY PARETO'S PRINCIPLE

Curiously, the relationship between urgency and importance was illuminated more than 100 years ago by the Italian economist Vilfredo Pareto (1848–1923). In 1897, Pareto discovered a relationship between inputs and outputs that has come to be known as the 80/20 rule, or the Pareto Principle. He found that 80 percent of what a person achieves is derived from 20 percent of the time the person expends. The key to effectiveness then is to continually identify the 20 percent of activities that are most important (that is, yield the greatest results).

CAUTION

On any given day, only about $\frac{1}{5}$ of what you do accounts for $\frac{4}{5}$ of what you achieve.

When the Pareto Principle was applied in business and industry, startling observations followed. Within an insurance agency, for example, 20 percent of the agents generally produced 80 percent of the sales. In a hardware store, 20 percent of the floor space accounted for 80 percent of the profits. In an accounting firm, 20 percent of the clients generated 80 percent of the revenues. It made sense for such firms to focus their energy on finding and keeping long-term, profitable clients.

DOUBLE YOUR PLEASURE

In his book, *The Secret to Achieving More With Less*, Richard Koch observes that you can identify where your company is getting back more than it is putting in, and then focus on that area and become highly profitable. Conversely, if you can figure out where your company is getting back much less than it is investing, you can reduce expenses or diminish losses considerably. Your mission becomes one of continuing to identify the important activities—those that yield the greatest desirable results.

TIP

Koch advises that when something is working well, double or redouble your efforts. If something isn't working so well, change course often and early rather than infrequently and late.

Even among successful people, most individuals don't sufficiently engage in the activities that would make them successful, even when they know what those activities are. Either by habit or by decree, they maintain a schedule that pretty much allocates the same time and effort to the same kinds of tasks, even though not all tasks provide the same contribution to desirable ends.

Think about the times in the last month or quarter when you were highly successful on the job. What elements were present? Could you map it all out? What 20 percent of those elements were crucial to your success?

THE FEW KEY FACTORS

Of the hundreds and hundreds of factors that could influence the impact of my presentation when I make keynote speeches to groups, a handful are of paramount importance. For example, the lighting must be excellent, the sound system must working well, and the temperature of the room has to be comfortable. If I take care of the handful of things that I know have the greatest impact on my success for that presentation, the odds are that everything will go well.

Sure, a host of other little things can crop up, but I could spend an inordinate amount of time trying to take care of everything. Instead, I focus on the handful of key factors that have proven themselves to be prominent. Likewise, in your own career, in big, long-duration goals as well as daily ones, you need to identify the handful of elements that need to be in place in order to dramatically increase your probability of success.

CAUTION

Too few career professionals spend enough time and thought on the handful of important factors that make a pronounced difference in what they are trying to achieve.

SYSTEMIZE, SYSTEMIZE, SYSTEMIZE

To make maximum use of your time, create simple but effective systems that accomplish what you want to accomplish without stressing your resources. The most ideal management system is that which works automatically with little or no input on your part.

TIP

> Never manage what you can eliminate altogether.

A dramatic example of this occurred years ago when steel magnate Andrew Carnegie hired a high-priced consultant to increase the productivity of workers in Carnegie's factory. The consultant came in, studied the factory workers, and studied their daily output. Then one Sunday evening, he took a piece of chalk and wrote a huge number six on the floor. As the day shift assembled on Monday, they saw the number and assumed that it was related to how many units the evening shift was able to produce. That day, they produced seven units, and before leaving, they crossed out the six and near it wrote the number seven.

That evening, the night shift saw the number seven, heard that that was how many units the day shift was able to produce, and set about to produce eight. Over the course of the next two weeks, the number of units produced increased markedly, leveled off a bit, and then became the new standard.

The consultant had done his job with a piece of chalk and an understanding of the factory and its workers. He had prompted a friendly competition between the day and night shift that resulted in a higher level of output thereafter.

BEYOND PARETO'S PRINCIPLE

Out of all the possibilities within your organization, what are the few key projects, the task forces, and the special teams you need to be on to propel your career? If you identify these and strive to be a part of them, you will benefit from the 80/20 rule!

PLAIN ENGLISH

Pareto's Principle   An observation about the relationship between inputs and outputs, essentially that 80
percent of one's effectiveness is derived from 20 percent of one's activities.

You need to have friends in your field and nurture them on a regular
basis. Without such allies, you're going to continually be reinventing
the wheel and skating over thin ice. With such allies on your side, you
catapult your career, transform your life, and accomplish so much
more than you thought before you knew them.

CAUTION

The larger your organization, the harder it is to be
successful entirely on your own.

Who are the few key players with whom you need to ally within your
organization? Yes, it pays to be on cordial terms with as many people
as you can, but who are the few key people with whom it is crucial? A
couple of co-workers? A mentor? A few people in another department?
Protégés? Some of the higher-ups in the organization?

The best relationships are those that are what author Robert Ringer
calls *value-for-value relationships.* Perhaps you give each other vital
information, have high respect for each other, or have a shared experience. Long-standing and winning relationships are based on trust,
reciprocity, and mutual enjoyment of each other's company. These
relationships develop over time; it's hard to take shortcuts.

PLAIN ENGLISH

Value-for-value relationship   The parties both offer
equally valuable or worthwhile contributions to one
another.

If you are new in your career, choose mentors who can open doors for you, point you in the right direction, and save you bundles of time that you may have otherwise expended heading down wrong paths. What value do mentors get associating with you? Prudent mentors know that protégés help to keep them in touch with the times and alert to new opportunities and new trends on the horizon. If you doubt this, think of the last time you learned something from your kids that you wouldn't ever have learned on your own.

WELCOME PARETO'S PRINCIPLE IN SMALL FIRMS

If you work in a service organization, what are the key ways you can most effectively serve clients or customers that would cause them to perceive a dramatic increase in value-added services? You can't be all things to all customers. If you attempt this, you are like the man who jumped on his horse and rode off in all directions.

These questions will help you focus on the subject and goals at hand:

- What can you offer faster and easier than anyone else?

- How can you carve out a niche for yourself?

- How can you position yourself in the minds of those you want to serve and serve them in a way such that they remain loyal to you?

To answer these questions, you have to study what the best in your industry do and improvise. Don't necessarily do exactly what they do; do something a little different, a little more innovative, a little better. The key is recognizing the few important things that you need to do and having the mental and emotional strength to let go of the rest.

CAUTION

If you try to do it all, you end up frustrated, anxious, and sometimes burned out.

Are you willing to use your time to concentrate on those elements of your career or your business that add the most value to your constituents? To do this, you need to know where the companies or organizations in your industries make healthy or even gargantuan profits. Constantly be on the lookout to uncover the 80/20 principles at play in your own industry. If you are already very good at something, and it is in demand, work harder to be even better at it.

Do you already have a focus area where you are more knowledgeable than anyone else? Then study it even further and become the leader. Identify all the ways to benefit from the Pareto Principle, capitalizing on your service or knowledge advantage so that you induce strong demand for your services, engender loyal clients or customers, or even have people seeking you out rather than vice versa.

THE 30-SECOND RECAP

- After you have identified what is important and urgent, you are better able to allocate your time more effectively.

- To consistently stay productive, focus on what is important and urgent and have the mental and emotional strength to stick with it.

- The Pareto Principle or 80/20 rule applies in many aspects of life, and in particular, it applies to your career. Identify the handful of activities in your career that produce the greatest results and watch your career soar.

- Identify the handful of key allies you need to have in your organization or within your career and have them help you achieve your best.

- Identify the handful of key service elements you can offer to clients or customers that will encourage them to remain loyal and prompt others to seek you out.

LESSON 4

Scheduling for Results

In this lesson, you will learn how to plan effectively so that important and urgent projects are accomplished on time.

THE FUNDAMENTALS REMAIN THE SAME

The ever-accelerating onslaught of new technology is constantly providing more and more tools to help you manage your time effectively. Today's planning software enables you to accomplish the following tasks:

- Manage your daily, weekly, and monthly schedules
- Align your daily activities with important and urgent tasks you face
- Plan projects
- Share files via downloads
- Electronically link your plans and schedules with others

With a palmtop computer, you can easily take your plans with you when you travel, maintain your database of contacts, send faxes, send and receive e-mail, and log onto the Internet (for more details see Lesson 8, "Taming Technology").

Despite the proliferation of these electronic and digital aids, however, the underlying components of effectively scheduling your time and making progress on selected tasks and projects remain the same. Any goal that you intend to achieve needs to be written down and quantified and has to have specific timeframes (as discussed in Lesson 3, "Avoiding the Tyranny of the Urgent"). If you don't have a timeline attached to a task or project, it probably will never get done.

Whether you use traditional, non-technical types of tools, such as hand-drawn charts or grids, or more sophisticated project management and scheduling software (on your desktop computer, notebook computer, or palmtop), you still need to plan. Carefully plotting the steps that lead to the desired result …

- greatly increases your probability of accomplishment.

- can contribute to greater productivity.

- is a fundamental concept in effective time management.

The basic three forms of project management and/or scheduling include milestone charts, flow charts, and calendars.

PLAIN ENGLISH

Gantt chart   A linear, visual tool for measuring progress made in pursuit of various activities over the course of time.

THE MILESTONE CHART METHOD

If you've ever been involved in any type of project management, you're probably already familiar with milestone charts, also known as Gantt charts. Milestone charts offer you an at-a-glance view of your progress on a variety of tasks and projects in relation to time, as shown in the following example:

	Month 1	Month 2	Month 3	Month 4	Month 5
Project 1	>>>>>>	>>>>>>>>>	>>>		
Project 2	>	>>>>>>	>>>>>>	>>>>>	
Project 3			>>>>>	>>>>>>>	
Project 4				>>>>>>>>>	>>

Milestone (Gantt) Chart

Here is how these charts work: Suppose one of your priorities is to continue to advance in your career. One of your goals in support of that priority is to get a raise of $6,000 at the next quarterly performance and appraisal session scheduled in 11 weeks. To support that goal, you've identified five projects that will greatly enhance the value of your services to your boss and the higher-ups in your division:

- Rewriting the orientation manual for new hires

- Getting an article published in one of the top three magazines in your industry

- Starting an online monthly newsletter for your firm's top clients and prospects

- Completing the DEF report three weeks earlier than it is due

- Participating at the key trade show, where you make important contacts and gather critical information for your boss

Adding these five accomplishments to your performance record over the next 11 weeks beyond what you already do in the normal course of the day and week will be challenging, but you feel up to it.

How can you allocate your time and resources so as to complete each of these projects with a flourish to thus position yourself for the salary increase that you are after? One way is to plot each of the activities on a weekly milestone chart so that you have a clear indication of the timeline and sequencing of each of these activities and support of your overall goal.

Item	1	2	3	4	5	6	7	8	9	10	11
Rewrite manual	>>	>>>>>	>>>>>	>>							
Publish article		>>>	>>			>>>>		>>>			
Online zine				>>>	>>>>>	>>>>>	>>>>>	>>>>>	>>>>>		
DEF report					>>	>>>	>>>				
Trade show							>>>	>			

Milestone Chart (in weeks)

To begin, you plot the most basic information for each project. Then, extending the process a bit further, you can even have subtasks under each task area. For example, in getting an article published, you may first have to interview some people or conduct some research. Then you might have to organize your notes, create an outline, and then write a first draft. Next, you would write your second draft, have peer review, go for a final draft, and then submit the article to the leading industry publications. Finally, you have to follow up to ensure that the publishers are paying attention to what you have written. A milestone chart with subtasks may look something like the following example:

Item	1	2	3	4	5	6	7	8	9	10	11
Rewrite manual	>>	>>>>>	>>>>>	>>							
Publish article											
Interviews		>>									
Research		>	>								
Organize			>								
Outline				>>							
First draft						>>					
Peer Review						>>					
Second draft							>>				
Submit								>			
Follow up											>
Online zine				>>>	>>>>>	>>>>>	>>>>>	>>>>>	>>>>>		
DEF report					>>	>>>	>>>				
Trade show							>>>	>			

Milestone Chart with Subtasks

You may have anywhere from 6 to 10 subtasks in pursuit of this task of getting an article published. The amount of detail is your choice. The important thing is that what you record is of value to you; it helps you to continue your progress toward your chosen goals. Likewise, with the other tasks, you may find yourself plotting anywhere from two or three subtasks to 15 or more.

CAUTION

> List the level of detail that will serve you and no more. If you unnecessarily complicate the chart, it will be counterproductive to your purposes.

You can enhance the chart by adding symbols such as a broken line that denotes the beginning of the project, numbers that refer to footnotes at the bottom of the chart, left and right arrows that indicate periods of activity, and so on. If the chart is on the wall, on a single piece of paper on a file folder, or on your hard drive, you can use colors to help guide you along as well. Green, for example, could mark the start of tasks. Yellow could indicate some critical function. Blue could represent completion.

TIP

> Write people's initials next to particular subtasks to represent the people whose cooperation is needed or perhaps to whom you will delegate the entire subtask.

Depending on the level of detail you are comfortable with, you could devise separate milestone charts for each task and carefully plot out all of the subtasks, assign start and stop times, use symbols to add detail, and use colors to denote progress. If you're working with different people on each task, then a separate milestone chart might make it easier for them. Similarly, when you consider the priority areas of your life and the goals you have selected in support of them, multiple milestone charts may suit you. However, you want to keep things as simple as possible.

THE FLOWCHART METHOD

Most people have had experience with flowcharts at one time or another. Perhaps your grade-school teachers used circles and squares connected by lines to depict the relationship between numbers, explain the migration of nomadic peoples, or illuminate the interaction of chemical compounds.

Although flowcharts are widely used to convey the essence of a process, they also can be used to do the following:

- Track project progress

- Help you stay on target

- Help you accomplish your goals

Flowcharts are particularly useful in plotting activities related to one task or project area where many different people or resources are required and contingencies come into play.

Flowcharts also allow for feedback loops. If the answer to a question is *yes,* the flowchart proceeds along one path; if the answer is *no,* it proceeds along another. For example, if an article is submitted to a publication and the editor wants specific changes, the feedback loop could encompass where you go next, such as back to your desk for rewrite, before resubmitting the article and continuing along the line you have already traversed, but this time having made improvements.

Flowcharts can extend downward or to the right. In business, they usually extend to the right so that a timeline can be added to the top or bottom of the chart, as shown in the following example.

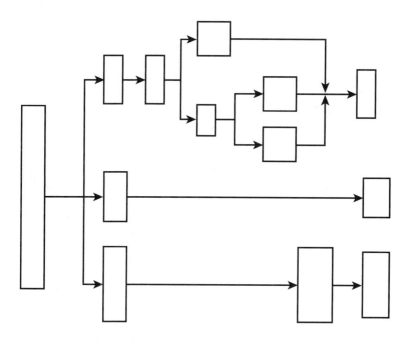

As with milestone charts, you can use colors and symbols to convey different types of information at a glance. For example, a triangle conveys a yes/no decision, a circle can be a connecting point, and squares offer information. A straight line represents a direct connection, a broken line is a partial or one-way connection, and a squiggly line indicates an interrupted or intermittent connection. You can draw symbols and lines in specific colors to convey another level of at-a-glance information. As always, remember to keep things simple.

TIP

Add a key at the bottom of the flowchart that shows exactly what each symbol and color represents.

THE CALENDAR METHOD

Using a calendar to ensure progress toward chosen goals is a time-honored method. Suppose one of your projects is to prepare a completely new orientation manual for new hires. This project must be completed by March 31, so you write "Complete manual" on the March 31 box on your calendar, as the following figure shows.

MARCH						
Sunday	Monday	Tuesday	Wednesday	Thursday	Friday	Saturday
	1	2	3	4	5	6
7	8	9 Initiate review	10	11	12	13
14	15 Proofread manual	16	17	18	19 Assemble copies	20
21	22 Schedule conference	23	24	25	26	27
28	29	30	31 Complete manual			

TIP

To make this system work, use calendar pages from the current year for however many months are relevant to the project you are managing.

Working from that end date of March 31 back to the present, you need to figure out what has to take place just before delivering the new orientation manual. For example, you need to meet with several department heads to offer your executive briefing and obtain their vital input at least a week before you turn in the manual. So you schedule a conference for March 22. Then you need to determine what has to happen before the conference.

In each case, plot the dates on the calendar, and then connect them with arrows that show the relationships of the dates. As in the case of milestone charts and flowcharts, you may use colors and symbols to give you a quick visual review of your progress.

Interestingly, with this calendar "block-back" method, you can quickly see that if you miss any interim date on the calendar, you will jeopardize the completion of the subtasks at the following interim dates. In essence, each interim date represents a mini-deadline. Hence, you have a nearly built-in system for ensuring that your project will continue according to plan.

TIP

For goals that stretch on for years or decades, starting with the end in mind is the only practical way to proceed.

The concept of starting with the end in mind and working backwards also works well in other goal areas you may have selected. Suppose that you want to retire by age 65 with $850,000, and you are currently 32 years old. By making basic assumptions about interest rates and inflation and taking taxes into account, you can numerically determine how much you would have to save per year or per month to achieve your desired end.

TIP

Milestone charts, flowcharts, and large wall calendars are available at office supply stores or office supply Web sites. You can also buy erasable charts to make course corrections easier.

SCHEDULING TOOLS FIT FOR THE PROS

More powerful, feature-laden scheduling software, calendar systems, and other project organizers become available with each passing month. All these scheduling aids offer some highly convenient common tools, including the following:

- A calendar system for tracking appointments, identifying schedule conflicts, and flagging areas and times of critical activity

- A variety of chart forms to choose from, including milestone charts, flowcharts, and calendars

- Drop-down menus, a drag-and-drop feature, and convenient icons

- The flexibility to add or subtract subtasks and activities in any desired sequence

- Colors, symbols, and other tools that offer at-a-glance information

- Alarms, bells, and buzzers that can be toggled on and off easily and set at certain times and intervals

- The ability to fax, e-mail, or download onto a Web site any chart file

- Multiple options for printing any chart

CAUTION

No matter how sophisticated the project manager or scheduling software you use is, it will be of little use if the information you are adding to it is not current or is inaccurate.

As with any planning or scheduling tool, someone has to be in the driver's seat. If you are not keeping up with the timelines you have established, particularly if you are sharing a scheduler with others, the schedule will quickly become ineffectual. Likewise, if you bite off more than you can chew, scheduling and planning tools may alert you to what you have done, but it is up to you to get back on track. In that respect, the most critical factor in planning and scheduling at all times is you!

The 30-Second Recap

- Milestone charts, flowcharts, and calendars are three of the most common types of scheduling tools. They offer a quick visual review of the sequence and interim progress toward completing tasks and projects in pursuit of a goal.

- Planning tools as part of a software program can easily be shared with others, making them ideal for team or group efforts.

- Any tool, whether manual or software-based, will break down the minute you don't keep it up-to-date.

LESSON 5
Getting Organized

In this lesson, you will learn the principles of personal organization that will enable you to accomplish more in less time with less stress.

ENTROPY IN YOUR OFFICE

Some people seem to be born organized. When you look at their desks, offices, cars, and homes, everything seems to be in its place. The way they schedule and complete projects or even make time for leisure seems to say, "I'm organized." Conversely, others seem to have a knack for disorganization. All the spaces in their lives seem to be cluttered. They never know where anything is.

However, being organized is not a matter of being born under a lucky star. Being personally organized involves learning a simple set of techniques and mastering a few basic skills.

PLAIN ENGLISH

Entropy That physical phenomena whereby everything, even the entire universe itself keeps expanding, keeps going forward.

Everything in the universe is subject to *entropy*. If you leave a field alone and come back several years later, the grass will be higher, weeds will abound, new plants will spring up. Indeed the natural state of planet Earth is abundance.

Likewise, if you leave a house empty and abandoned for 10 years, the house will be subject to entropy. The yard will be overgrown. Cracks will start to show up in the foundation or elsewhere. The paint would begin to chip. The roof might leak, and bricks in the chimney might come loose. However, when people live in the house and a little thing goes wrong, they fix it; they continually restore the house to operable condition.

 CAUTION

> Like an untreated cavity can lead to a root canal, a little clutter can become a big problem if you ignore it.

Entropy is alive and well on your hard drive, on your desk, on your shelf, and in all the spaces of your life. In this day and age, when we are all subject to so much information coming at us, piles can accumulate quickly. These piles might include documents, reports, newspapers, bills, magazines, certificates, you name it.

CAUTION

> Piles by their very nature represent disorganization.

It is hard to manage stuff stacked up in a pile. Many organizational experts contend that accumulations represent a basic lack of decision-making capability. In other words, you have piles of stuff because you haven't decided what to do with the stuff in the first place.

If you have been following the lessons in this book sequentially, you know from Lesson 2, "Shaping Your Future," that identifying your priorities and establishing goals in support of those priorities can help you to better use your time and to stay more focused and more directed. Likewise, priorities and goals also help you to have a clear handle on what to do when stuff comes your way.

Those individuals with the most highly refined set of priorities and most well-developed goals are more likely to have fewer piles and less clutter confronting them. Why? Because they know where things go as soon as they encounter them. Better still, as you learned from Lesson 1, "Understanding Time Management," they eliminate the possibility of most pieces of paper coming to their desks to begin with.

PILED HIGH BUT NOT HOPELESS

If you find yourself continually confronted with clutter, take heart. The situation is not hopeless. First, gather all the tools and accoutrements you will need to break down those piles or disband that clutter. These tools may include file folders, rubber bands, paper clips, staplers, boxes, and so on. In Lesson 6, "Managing Your Desk and Office," I will get into the details of managing your workspace so you will be able to find things easily. For now, recognize that piles and clutter don't magically go away, just as they didn't magically accumulate.

Allow yourself 30 minutes or, if that's too much, 15 minutes to go through each item in the pile and assess what to do with it. In essence, you can only do one of four things with the stuff that confronts you:

- Act on it.
- Delegate it.
- File it.
- Recycle it.

Of any given pile of stuff on your desk, chances are most of it can be recycled. You don't need to hang on to it. A lesser portion can probably be filed, and a slightly lesser portion of that can probably be delegated. That leaves you with a thin file of things to act on.

TIP

By categorizing the various items in your pile, you stand a better chance of whittling out the unnecessary items, and dealing with the rest becomes a more manageable task.

Don't spend too much time thinking about which group to place each item in; make a quick assessment and go on to the next item. After you have placed everything into its group, you will notice undoubtedly that the recycle group is the largest. The file group, hopefully, is much smaller. The group of stuff to delegate to other people is smaller still, and the group of things you need to act on should be the smallest of all.

Go through the items you need to act on and rank them according to what is most important. If an item is both urgent and important (see Lesson 3, "Avoiding the Tyranny of the Urgent"), put it on top of the group. If an item is important but not urgent, place it next. If it is simply urgent, place it after that, and if it is neither urgent nor important, recycle it, file it, or delegate it.

After you have determined which items or tasks are urgent and important, rank those items as well. Research has confirmed that when you have multiple items competing for your time and attention, ranking them according to their importance and working on each item in order until it is completed is the fastest and most efficient way to tackle the tasks or projects facing you.

 PLAIN ENGLISH

Clutter   An unorganized accumulation of items, the collective value of which is suspect.

SUPPORTING PRINCIPLES

Any time you face a pile or clutter in general or feel disorganized, keep in mind the following principles:

- **Recycling:** Identifying items for recycling (chucking) is usually easiest. You want to get your pile to a lean and mean state; by chucking things at high speed, you have the best chance.

- **Order of importance or urgency**: Frequently downgrade the status of items as you see fit. If you have too many items in your important file, you are stuck with the same problem you had before you dealt with the pile. Everything seems to be competing for your time and attention with equal fervor. If you can successfully downgrade the status of an item (for example, from important and urgent to simply important or simply urgent or to something that someone else can handle), then you have reduced the immediate burden that you face.

- **Classification**: Continue to look for what can be combined, automated, systemized, delegated, delayed, ignored, or used for fireplace kindling.

- **Organization**: When you have pared down piles to the least possible volume, use whatever tools you have available (rubber bands, paper clips, file folders, and so on) to keep them neat and orderly.

TIP

The more like things that you can group together, the easier it will be to deal with them. Also, the easier it will be to see duplicates that you can recycle or discard.

Make a game of staying organized: Continually look for backsides of pieces of paper that are reusable for rough drafts and copies and keep an eye out for items that someone else might appreciate but that you don't really need to retain.

TIP

If something you are holding on to can truly help another person, it will be far easier for you to give it away.

TACKLING THE IMPORTANT PILE

When you're ready to begin working on the items in your important group, list them all and make an estimate of how long it will take to complete each item. Then add all the estimates together and multiply that number by 1.5. This amount compensates for your underestimation. Let's face it: Things often take longer than we think they will. We don't know how long a project will take until we do it, at which point all kinds of other issues sometimes arise.

If the number of task hours facing you to complete the important tasks grows to an astronomical figure, don't get overly concerned. At least you now have more accurate information regarding the challenge facing you.

Now, marshal your resources. Realistically, what will it take to accomplish all that you have laid out before you as important and urgent, important, and so on? You may need additional staff help, a bigger budget, or, in the short run, a longer workday.

 TIP

Sometimes you can't complete a task because certain steps are dependent on others. Take it as far as you can go, and then consult with others. During the interim, start on the next project.

Now and then, no matter how methodical your approach or well-organized your desk and office are, new items will compete for your time and attention and conspire to upset your perfectly arranged kingdom. This is going to happen on a daily, if not hourly, basis. In Lesson 6, I will explain how to arrange your office, desk, and files so as to be able to accommodate the influx of new materials.

MIX IT UP

As time passes, you'll find that you need a break from working on the important tasks that you have so carefully arranged. You can give your rapt attention and earnest efforts to the primo projects for only so long, and then your mind starts to wander. You need a mental break.

At this point, feel free to turn to items far lower down on the pile that still require your attention, but don't require so much mental effort. Give yourself a 10-, 15- or 20-minute run on lower-level items that are less mentally taxing. When you feel ready, turn back to the most important items.

KEEPING IT IN PERSPECTIVE

You already know that smaller piles are easier to manage than larger ones. Hence, your goal should be to continue to keep your piles as slim and trim as possible, although there are exceptions that I will discuss shortly. Reduce the weight and volume of each pile by retaining only the highly relevant information and nothing more. For example, rather than retaining a 10-page report, hang on to only the single page that you need.

Taking that principle further, if you only need one paragraph, phone number, address, or Web site on a page, then clip that portion and recycle the rest of the page. Attach the small clipping that you have retained to a sheet that contains other small, relevant tidbits, and then photocopy the page. You now have a dossier page that fully supports what you are working on, but doesn't take up much space physically or psychologically.

Sometimes it does pay to let piles or accumulations mount up. When you receive a plethora of like items, it is okay to let the pile grow temporarily. Perhaps a stack of everything related to the competitor's product is accumulating in the corner of that table in your office. That's okay because the pile is temporary and you intend to handle it completely in short order.

When that sacred time arrives, delve into the pile like a buzz saw. Immediately discard duplicate information. Combine like items, and then consider which of those items can be recycled as well. Pare down so that you have the slimmest, most potent pile possible.

When the pile is reasonably thin, look at it once more and ask yourself what else can be thrown away. What items represent something that you already know quite well, but you are holding on to as an information crutch? Don't be surprised to find that you can reduce the file by yet another 33 percent.

TIP

> If you have several slimmed-down piles, arrange them in a stair-step fashion down one side of your desk. This arrangement allows you to quickly withdraw any particular pile in the arrangement while keeping the others in order.

A PSYCHIC REWARD

I've discussed the issue of getting organized with top achievers in many different professions. Each agrees that when his or her desk or office and personal surroundings are in order, he or she feels far more energized at the start of the day. Conversely, when these top achievers come into their offices at the start of the day and see a huge mess, they feel somewhat defeated.

From the standpoint of managing your time and staying organized, as well as feeling energized, clear your desk and surroundings each evening as you end work for the day so that the next day you can be at your best. When you leave with a clear desk, you give yourself a sense of closure or completion to your day. This sense of completion gives you a greater chance to enjoy the rest of your evening.

PLAIN ENGLISH

> **Being organized**   Arranging one's possessions, time, or life, so as to remain comfortably in control.

When you arrive in the morning and are greeted by a clear, clean surrounding, you gain a psychological boost much as the high achievers did. What's more, you are automatically drawn to the most important issue, or you get to make a fresh decision about what materials to extract from your desk, filing cabinet, or shelves based on what you want to accomplish that morning. This situation is far different than merely dealing with what you left on the desk the night before.

TIP

> Some projects span several days and in that sense, it can be prudent on occasion to simply leave a file folder open on your desk so that it will greet you the next morning. However you don't want to fall into the habit where you are always being greeted by stuff you left on the desk the night before.

When you begin each morning with a clear, clean desk and clear, clean office and focus on tasks that you deem most important and urgent at that time, you work with more energy, more focus, and more direction. You tend to get things done in less time overall, because you begin working right away on the thing that you deem is most important. You also experience less stress.

EXTENDING THE NOTION

Getting organized in your personal life supports your efforts in your professional life. The more organized you are at home, in your car, and in the other places in your life, the greater the probability that you will have more focus, energy, and direction when you head to work. You will certainly be more efficient and perhaps have greater piece of mind.

At home, if your closets are jammed with stuff you have been stowing since you moved into the house, it's time to engage in spring cleaning, whether spring is here or not. If you can't bear to part with all the stuff you crammed in there, at least separate it by the seasons.

TIP

> As spring approaches, box up all the winter items and put them in the attic, basement, or some infrequently used room. It should take you 60 minutes or less for each closet.

As you go through your house reclaiming spaces, you will find the pay-off spills over into your career. Twenty-first century men and women are inundated with too many items competing for their time and attention at work, at home, and in between. Just as cramming too many activities into a given unit of time tends to make that time speed by perceptually, cramming too many items into a physical space tends to make one feel somewhat out of control. By reclaiming spaces, you can find things faster and easier, which saves time and makes it easier to get out of the house in the morning and stow things at the end of the day.

FROM HOME TO OFFICE AND BACK AGAIN

The fastest and easiest way to maintain order in your home and have that principle spread to your office is to defend your borders. That means you must semi-fanatically guard your home and your life so that no extraneous items enter to begin with. Similar to limiting the number of the pieces of paper that cross your desk at work, you want to limit the number of items that come into your home and make their way onto your shelves. At work, you want to keep your flat surfaces relatively clear and leave ample room in your filing cabinets, on your shelves, and in other spaces around your office (more on this in Lesson 6).

THE 30-SECOND RECAP

- Though personal organizational skills aren't handed out at birth, people who are organized and stay organized practice some specific behaviors that people who are disorganized don't do.

- Any pile that you face, particularly on your desk, can be pared down in 30 minutes or less. Most of what you face can be recycled, a lesser amount can be filed, many items can be delegated, and generally, a few items will need to be worked on.

- Getting organized takes some time, but the payoff is worth it! To get organized in the office requires assembling the tools that will help you keep like items together.

- Getting organized at home ultimately supports your career organization efforts. Cleaning up your closets, drawers, and shelf space pays off in all aspects of your life.

LESSON 6

Managing Your Desk and Office

In this lesson, you will learn how to arrange your office, desk, working materials, and files so that you can find things quickly and easily.

STARTING AT THE TOP

When you arrange your office for high productivity, start with your desk, specifically with your desktop. You have to treat your desktop as sacred space. Everything on your desktop has to be there for a reason and must be positioned precisely to support the way you work.

No one is going to help you manage your desk or desktop. If you have a mentor or co-worker who is a pro at organization, then consider yourself among the fortunate few. If not, you have to roll up your sleeves and learn by trial and error. You already know from the previous lesson that if you have one project, one file folder, or one of whatever you're working on in front of you and the rest of your desk is clutter free, you are going to have …

- more energy.
- more focus.
- more direction.

What precisely do you need to have on your desktop? A quick answer is anything that you use on a recurring and daily basis. This could include a pen, a roll of tape, a stapler, a staple remover, Post-It pads, a ruler, and paper clips. Anything that you can't use on a daily or recurring basis does not belong on your desktop. Such items are best stored in a drawer within your desk or possibly a table or credenza in your office.

Why bother to make the distinction between what you use on a daily or recurring basis versus what you don't? Because your goal at all times is to have as few things on your desk as possible so that you will have as much open space as possible. You need open space and clear, clean, flat surfaces because more information will be coming onto your desk each day, each week, and each year of your career.

TIP

Establish a disembarking area where you can open packages, break down mail, or otherwise diminish piles of stuff.

IT'S WHAT'S INSIDE THAT COUNTS

Inside your desk you want to retain items that you use at least on a weekly basis, although items used daily can be stored there as well if they are particularly large or bulky. Recognize, however, that your desk drawers are not for storing supplies per se. You may store a pad of paper, but not pads of paper. You need only one pad at a time, and the general principle is to have the minimum amount of an item that you need, but then have no more.

TIP

Keep pads of paper and other supplies in a file folder, a storage locker, or further away from the epicenter of your creative and productive post.

When you have only those things on your desktop that ought to be on your desktop and only those things in your desk that ought to be there, proceed to the other storage compartments around your office. If you choose to use one of your desk drawers to contain file folders, then these file folders should contain only current projects. Also, they should be arranged in the fashion discussed in Lesson 5, "Getting Organized." The important and urgent materials come first, and the least important and least urgent materials are last. These files should be as thin and potent as you can make them.

TIP

Routinely discard extraneous information and be on the lookout for reducing, shrinking, and paring down where you can. Retain only the materials that are essential to retain.

WHAT TO SHELVE

Undoubtedly, you have some kind of shelves in your office. The question of what should be housed on your shelves versus what is best contained in a filing cabinet is relatively easy to answer. Shelves are best used to do the following:

- Temporarily store items you will use within 10 to 15 days.

- Store items that are too large to go in a filing cabinet.

- Hold a collection of like items, such as 12 issues of the same magazine in an upright magazine storage box.

- Contain current projects, the total contents of which you don't necessarily have to have on your desk.

- Store books, directories, supply catalogs, and other items with spine labels.

CAUTION

Make sure you allocate items you are temporarily storing on shelves in 10 to 15 days. When a temporary pile becomes a permanent pile, you begin to lose control of what you're retaining.

Be careful when you store elements of a project in progress on your shelves. It's fine to temporarily park the brunt of materials you are working with so that you can have just a few materials in front of you at any given time. However, if you're maintaining complete control of your desk, your shelves, and the project at hand, then ideally the materials should rotate from the desk to the shelf and back to your desk, become thinner in the progress, and eventually *not* appear on your shelves at all.

LIGHTEN THE LOAD

As more and more material comes into your office, you'll find it's easy to fill up your shelves in record time. With all the office supply catalogs, annual directories, software instruction guides, and company policy and procedure manuals, what was once an open space can quickly turn into a "no vacancy" situation.

To maximize shelf space, keep supplies in a supply cabinet. Ideally your supply cabinet is further away from your desk than your shelves. Supply cabinets are designed to house items in bulk. The goal in using supply cabinets is to be able to readily find what you need when you open them. Keeping like items together makes items easier to find. These items might be stacked on top of one another, horizontally, or end-to-end. Although you arrange items on your shelves with precision, supply cabinets allow for a lot more leeway.

 TIP

Extreme neatness is not necessary in a supply cabinet. However, the bigger the office staff sharing the supply cabinet is, the more important neatness becomes.

EVERYTHING IS CONNECTED

Highly organized individuals know that the relationship between one's desk, shelves, and supply cabinet is not static. What is housed in one location at one point in time ultimately may be housed somewhere else depending on the following factors:

- The tasks at hand

- The available resources to meet those tasks

- The timeframe for completing the tasks

At all times, you want to be on the prowl for items that can be tossed or recycled. If you don't need it, it's not worth filing or storing.

Too many people feel fearful about tossing items because they just know they will need it someday. But the truth is that tossing something out and then discovering you need it later may not be the major problem you imagine. Almost any list, report, or document that you can name can be replaced. Somebody else has a copy, it's on the Internet, or it's on somebody's hard drive. Not being able to think of a good reason to hang on to something is a good reason to toss it.

Professional organizers claim that as much as 80 percent of what executives retain at work never again sees the light of day. Even if they are off by 25 percent to 50 percent in their estimates, it still means that much of what you are hanging on to is dead wood! The more you have cleared out of your office, the easier it is to find what you've retained.

PAPER IS STILL KING

Despite the long-standing promise that we'll all be working in "paperless offices," most career professionals today are plagued by even more paper than their predecessors of a generation ago. If you analyze your most repetitive tasks, chances are that handling paper would be on the top of the list on most given days. In many respects, time management is synonymous with paper handling. Your mission is to whittle out all those pages of catalogs, magazines, and other voluminous work that come your way so that you deal only with what you need and nothing more.

TIP

> Reduce the potential for disorganization by dealing with paper right away when you get the mail, when somebody hands you something, or when you see something in your in basket after returning from being away.

Here are some paper-reducing ideas:

- Use your copy machine as often as possible to capture the few pages you need from a book or large document. Get rid of the part you don't need.

- Use a scanner to put key paragraphs and pages on your hard drive, where they are searchable and retrievable via your word processing program. This method is superior to filing something and then trying to find it on your own.

CAUTION

> Don't make the mistake of scanning indiscriminately, or you'll fill up your hard drive as quickly as you filled up your filing cabinets. Electronic disorganization is as anxiety-provoking as the manual kind.

- Use a junk drawer as a holding bin when stuff comes in too fast or when you're in the middle of an important project. Later, when the dust dies down, go to your junk drawer and whittle out as much as you can. Use the four-step process in assessing and allocating where the items should go: Act on it, delegate it, file it, or recycle or toss it.

TIP

> The act-on-it pile should always be the smallest. Rank the items in that pile according to what is important and urgent heading down to what is unimportant and not urgent.

Asking yourself the following series of questions can help you quickly determine what to do with the next item that crosses your desk:

- What does this document represent?

- Do I have to retain this at all?

- Who else should know about this?

- What if I don't do anything?

If an item you receive merits your attention and requires that you get in touch with someone, use the path of least resistance to resolve the issue. Determine whether you can ...

- fax instead of mail

- e-mail instead of fax

- pay by credit card instead of by check

- call instead of visit

CONTINUALLY BE ON THE LOOKOUT

Throughout the day, when the spirit moves you, examine your desktop, desk drawers, shelves, filing cabinet, and any storage cabinet to determine what, if anything, no longer needs to be retained. Outdated directories, instruction manuals, flyers, annual reports, brochures, public relations materials, announcements, catalogs, and invitations can all be tossed. Chuck the excess vendor supply catalogs that you may have on hand, duplicate items, annual reports that you don't look at, software you received in the mail that you are never going to explore, and take-out menus from restaurants you no longer frequent. Feel free to throw out old editions of books that you won't open again, back issues of magazines you haven't touched for more than a year, and bottles of correction fluid that have dried solid.

TIP

Get rid of scraps, rough drafts, memos, correspondence, reports, and any other documents that do not have to be retained.

THE NUTS AND BOLTS OF FILING

Filing is the ultimate organizational tool. When you file items effectively, you enable yourself to efficiently withdraw what you need when you need it. As author Jim Cathcart says, "Filing is not about storing; it is about retrieval." You file things either because they will help you to be prosperous in the future (for example, the information you retain has power) or because there are penalties for not filing them (for example, you won't be able to complete your taxes). The items that you file, therefore, should have potential future value.

CAUTION

If it has been a long time since you have reorganized your files, you are probably facing a gargantuan task. Nevertheless, this task is one that is well worth undertaking.

Rather than try to redo your entire filing cabinet, tackle one half of one drawer every week. This pace is safe and sane. Assemble the tools you'll need to be effective, such as several blank file folders, file folder labels, magic markers, color-coded dots, paper clips, fasteners, and such.

Rather than using two- or three-cut manila folders, splurge and buy black, green, pink, orange, or blue folders. Color-coded files help you to find things more quickly and easily. Think of the last time you were in your doctor's or dentist's office. If their patient files were exposed and in view, chances are you saw some kind of color-coded filing system. This system enables the people in the office to go right to the appropriate area, which cuts down the time searching for any particular file. You could use green file folders for anything that has to do with, say, money, blue for anything that has to do with your career progression, yellow for anything related to taxes, and so on.

Grab the first file in the first drawer you have chosen to tackle. Examine its contents:

- What can be chucked?

- What can be combined?

- What needs to be reallocated?

- What color folder or what color label will you use to house the remaining materials, knowing what you now know?

Everything in the file is subject to being combined, deleted, or moved around. Your goal at all times is to ensure that the things that you have chosen to file are housed in their best possible location.

Go to the second file in the drawer and allocate its contents as you will. If you're not sure that something is worth retaining, chances are it's not worth retaining. Management expert Edwin Bliss says, "When in doubt, throw it out."

 TIP

Because most of us keep more than is necessary, chances are you can pare down your files significantly and not suffer any negative consequences. And the less you have, the easier it is to find what you need.

When you have gone through the half-drawer for this particular session, relax, give yourself a break, and go do something else. You don't have to tackle the second half of the drawer until a week or so from now.

FEWER FILES, MORE IN THEM

At all times, you want to have fewer large files of like items as opposed to a number of smaller files. Why? You'll find it far easier to extract what you are looking for if you have to deal with only a few large files to begin with. Any search you do begins with the right file. It will then take you time to go through that file to find the particular document, but your odds of success will be high.

Conversely, if you have dozens and dozens of small files, you might not extract the correct file in three or four tries. If you are lucky and you do extract the correct file, the time required to extract the desired page within the file won't be that much quicker than extracting the desired page from a larger file.

PLAIN ENGLISH

Date stamping   The process of fixing a date to items as they arrive, and preferably before they are filed.

Some organizational experts swear by date stamping. Every time something goes into your file you stamp the corner of it indicating on what day it was placed in the file. If you're comfortable with doing this, go ahead. Keep in mind that an item's importance is not necessarily related to the date in which you filed it, although the longer an item has sat in your files without ever being used, the higher the probability is that you can safely chuck it.

FILE HEADINGS ARE THE KEY

What you file and how you file is largely governed by your file headings, which are the labels you place on the tab section of each file folder. It is easy enough to label one file folder Office Supplies, and another Insurance, and another New Technology. However, you probably want to be more creative than that to accommodate the variety of stuff that comes your way. Some of it appears worth retaining, at least in the short run, but it doesn't seemingly have a proper home. You could label your file folders with the following headings:

- Review After the First of the Year

- Hold Until After the Merger

- Check in a Month

- Check Next Spring

- Don't Know Where to File

By having a file labeled Don't Know Where to File, you automatically create a home for the handful of things that your instincts tell you to retain but that don't fit with anything else that you're doing. Now at least you have a fair chance of getting your hands back on such items when, lo and behold, the time might be right to reread the items closely.

TIP

If you're worried that a file labeled Don't Know Where to File may grow too large too quickly, remember that you can easily review its contents at any time and decide what to do with them.

LOCATING TICKLER FILES

As I describe at length in my book, *The Complete Idiot's Guide to Managing Your Time* (Macmillan, 1999), setting up a daily and monthly rotating tickler (reminder) file provides big benefits. Suppose something crosses your desk in March that looks interesting, but you don't have to act on it until April 25. If you have one file folder for each month of the year, you can park the item in the April folder.

Going further, you set up an additional 31 file folders marked 1, 2, and so on all the way up to 31 for the days in the month. Now, when April approaches, you open up the April file folder, take out all the contents and allocate them to file folders 1 through 31 as appropriate. Stick the now-empty April file folder at the end of the pack so that the month of May is now in front, preceded by file folders 1 through 31.

TIP

These 43 file folders (1 through 31 and January through December) enable you to park anything in the appropriate place when the item doesn't have to be dealt with too soon.

If you receive something on the third day of the month but don't have to deal with it until the eighteenth, put it in the folder marked 18, or better yet, give yourself some slack and put it in a folder two or three days before the eighteenth.

The tickler file provides a home for much of the clutter and stuff on your desk and around your office, because you've determined a date when you're going to review the materials. They are off your desk, off your counters, and off your mind. Yet you haven't lost them, you have just parked them in a location where you'll be able to retrieve them when you need to.

TIP

You can use a tickler file to write out your checks and pay your bills, and then store the envelopes in the folder that's prior to their due dates.

Many people who use tickler files find it convenient to review them at the start of each week and perhaps one or two more times during that week. One of the benefits of this process is that when you review the item days, weeks, or a month after first putting it in the tickler file, you often have a greater sense of objectivity. Choosing to act on the item, delegate it, file it again, or toss it becomes easier. Happily, much of what you review will be tossed. Having less clutter means you have greater organization and greater focus and direction on the pressing tasks that you face.

CREATING FILES IN ADVANCE OF THE NEED

A variation of the theme of employing both file labels and using tickler files is to create files in advance of when you need to store anything in them. Suppose you've decided that you absolutely want to work in the London office of your company by the end of next year. Perhaps you haven't even announced your intentions to anyone. Nevertheless, place a file in your filing cabinet labeled London.

Hereafter, every time you see something about London, you now have a home for it. Maybe you encounter documents from the London office. Maybe you find something related to travel in London. Later, perhaps you come across something related to housing in England.

Creating a file folder in advance of having anything to put into the folder is an affirmation of the goals you have chosen. At the least, it helps to keep you organized. If you don't have such a folder, where the heck are you going to put items relating to this goal? On top of something else where it will get buried by yet something else?

By extending the principle, you can create several file folders in advance of having anything to put into them, based on what priorities you have identified and what goals you have established in support of those priorities. Here are some ideas for file folders for this category:

- Retirement Villages

- Vacation to Bali

- Daycare Centers

- Palmtop computers

- Vision Correction

- Scholarships

ORGANIZE YOUR HARD DRIVE

The concept of filing is no less valid when it comes to your hard drive. There may be six or so file folders you don't need to create, but that would be most appropriate for you to create based on where you are heading in your career and your life.

TIP

When you create an empty file folder on your hard drive, especially off of another folder that you visit often, you are frequently reminded that you have a home to park files as they emerge for this new topic area.

If you supervise a staff, electronic filing can work particularly well. Create a file folder for each staff person, using his or her name. Thereafter, when you come across anything that needs to go into Erika's folder, drag it over and park it there. As time passes, and it's time for Erika to tackle another assignment, you flip open the directory, see what's in the hopper, and delegate accordingly.

You can even create a file folder for yourself on your hard drive called In Progress that you open at the start of each day, or a shortcut to such a folder on your desktop. The possibilities are endless! The point is for you to create space to house that which is worth housing so that you can quickly and easily retrieve what you need.

THE 30-SECOND RECAP

- Look upon managing your desk, shelves, filing cabinet, and storage cabinet as the means to an end, the end being that you are far more efficient in the use of your time.

- Your continual quest is to whittle out that which you do not need to retain and continually revisit your files and holdings to further pare down. You want to stay lean and mean. You want your files to be thin and potent.

- Rather than seeing filing as drudgery, consider it as an effective tool for storing items that contribute to your future prosperity or at least help you avoid penalties.

LESSON 7

Surviving Information Overload

In this lesson, you will learn how to limit the amount of information that confronts you while ensuring that you are exposed to issues critical to your job and personal well-being.

HOW BAD IS IT?

You have only to log onto the Internet, switch on the television, walk into a magazine store, or open your e-mail file to be deluged by information. The aggregate volume of information generated on Earth in a single minute exceeds what you could absorb in the next 80 years of your life, should you live that long. The next minute, the process repeats itself. No one can possibly keep up with the volume of information confronting humankind.

To effectively manage your time, set up filters in all aspects in your life so that you have access to information that you want or need to be exposed to but are not subject to the floodgate levels of information plaguing so many others. When you make active choices regarding the information you want to receive versus allowing yourself to be simply inundated, you set yourself up for success. You have charted a course unlike so many others who have never stopped and decided what information they want to be exposed to versus what information they simply are exposed to. This key distinction will sustain your career for decades to come.

You can't subscribe to all the top magazines, read all the latest books, and attend all the big symposiums. Thus, you have to draw upon the Pareto Principle (see Lesson 3, "Avoiding the Tyranny of the Urgent"), recognizing that about 20 percent of the information to which you are exposed yields 80 percent or more of the insights, key facts, and essential knowledge that will propel you in your efforts.

So you ask, "How do I identify that important 20 percent?" It is easier than you might think. If there are several magazines, journals, and newsletters within your profession, chose the two or three that represent the leading sources and have the most in-depth coverage, the largest research staff, and the best writing.

KEEP PACE WITH YOUR CLIENTS

Beyond reading what your top peers read, you also want to discover the top industry journals read by your clients, customers, or constituents. After all, the organization that employs you serves some type of constituent, whether they are called customers, clients, patients, or consumers. Find out what these people read, identify the few key publications, and subscribe to those as well.

By receiving the same information that the top people whom you are trying to serve receive, you begin to understand the issues that confront them, the terminology, the players, and all facets of their world. You are honing in on the key bits of information that will help you to understand what it takes to serve your constituency. What could be more efficient?

CAUTION

> Far too many career professionals are steeped in the information of their own industry but forget to take the vital step of reading what their clients read.

As you read articles and news briefs related to your constituents, fill your file folders and hard drive space with information you can draw upon, massage, combine, and use to even better serve your clients and customers. When you're in face-to-face meetings, on the phone, or delivering correspondence to your constituents, the quality of your message will be higher because you have taken the time and effort to delve into the information that defines their world.

GETTING OTHERS TO SIFT FOR YOU

What if someone could sift through information for you and act as a filter so that you receive only the essence of voluminous amounts of information that you might otherwise be tempted to weed through yourself? Although not many people use this technique, you can have somebody else serve as your information scout.

PLAIN ENGLISH

> **Prereader**   Someone who serves as an information scout for another, paring down voluminous reading materials to their essence.

Look around your office and around your home. If you are the type of person who routinely amasses piles of reading materials, then you could use a *prereader*. Rather than continually feel swamped by too much information, delegate somebody, hire somebody, or enlist one of your children to read through materials for you.

How does this work? Although I will explore multiplying your time through delegation in Lesson 10, "Multiplying Your Time Through Delegation," for now, consider that if you can offer clear instructions on what type of information you're seeking and how you want it to be presented, someone else can wade through those key chapters in the latest book, that stack of magazines you have been accumulating, and those reports piling up on the corner of your desk. The key is to draw up a roster of essential terms and phrases, key themes, and key issues that you want the prereader to flag. Perhaps you want the prereader to copy any page where a key issue appears or underline key paragraphs.

 TIP

> By properly conveying what you want when you delegate your reading material and choosing the right person to be your prereader, you can dramatically cut down the amount of information you are exposed to and increase the speed with which you can take action on information.

Begin by giving your prereader some light assignments. For example, after he or she has followed your instructions in reviewing a particular magazine, scan the entire magazine as you normally would have done without a prereader. This will help you assess how close your prereader was to identifying the few key sections that are important to you.

Be sure to give your prereader detailed feedback following the first several assignments. As he or she begins to exhibit increasing capability for highlighting and underscoring precisely those articles and passages that you would have selected yourself, increase the scope of your assignments.

Regardless of what you assign, having a prereader doesn't prevent you from reading things on your own that you choose not to delegate. However, as you learn to trust the judgment of your prereader, increasingly you'll find that it is far more efficient to have him or her sift through more and more of what you would have spent hours going through. Suppose your prereader is finished going through a magazine for you. He or she is now a veteran of selecting what you want. You still can quickly read over other things that the prereader may not have highlighted, yet you find yourself being able to delve into the preselected materials that the prereader found for you at record speeds.

Remember, you can absorb and, more importantly, apply only so much of the information that you are exposed to. When a prereader whittles down large volumes of information so that what is left is fertile, you've not only saved a great deal of time and storage space, but you have also set up an environment where you are more easily able to act on the few things highlighted for your attention.

You're Not Done Yet

Continue to look for other easy ways to handle all the information that competes for your time and attention. Instead of reading voluminous amounts of materials that someone else in your office has already read, have him/her brief you.

TIP

> If you discuss information with a co-worker or friend who has read what you want to read, you may not have to read the original subject matter yourself.

You may have heard the story about Franklin D. Roosevelt. One of his advisors brought him a 100-page report on some current, crucial topic. Roosevelt looked at it and said, "This is far too much for me to go through. Can you boil it down?" The advisor came back in a day or two with a 10-page executive summary. Roosevelt looked at it for a few seconds and said, "Still too much. Boil it down." The advisor, very miffed, came back after a couple hours with one page of key notes. Roosevelt looked at the page and said, "Come on, man, I'm busy; boil it down." The advisor came back in a half-hour with a single paragraph. Roosevelt's eyes darted over it for a moment. Then, he looked up at the advisor and said, "Can you give it to me in a sentence?"

CONTINUE TO PRUNE YOUR FILES

The time and effort that you spend whittling out what you no longer need pays off in many ways. For one, you physically have the space both within your desk and file cabinets and on your hard drive to accommodate new information, which, as we know by now, is on its way. Chucking what you don't need to hang on to also gives you the opportunity to review that which you have filed and choose to retain. Sometimes the information that you filed months ago combined with something you just learned adds up to new knowledge on which you can capitalize.

 CAUTION

> The tendency to hang on to too much information is endemic to early twenty-first-century man and woman. Keep asking yourself, "Do I really need to retain this?"

Here are some good places to look for material you no longer need:

- Clean out your database. There are contacts in your database who have left the area or perhaps passed away or who you know you will never call on again. Delete them without remorse from your database.

- Review your files. Toss out every piece of paper in your files that represents issues that are neither important, urgent, or, for that matter, even interesting. Keep the others in the aforementioned holding bins (see Lesson 6, "Managing Your Desk and Office.")

- Eliminate files on your hard drive that were once able to capture your attention, but now, after months or perhaps years, have overstayed their welcome.

- Examine your office at large. Have you collected business cards of people you know whom you will never call back? Are there gifts and mementos that you have received that hold little meaning for you or take up more space than they are worth? Are there book reports and documents that are no longer (or have yet to be) useful? If so, throw them out!

CHART YOUR PROGRESS

The following chart, adapted from my book, *The Joy of Simple Living*, offers a quick and easy guide for what to retain versus what to toss:

Items	Toss or Recycle If ...	Retain If ...
Business cards	You have many cards and never call anyone, or you can't recall the person or his goods or services.	You already have a cardholder, can scan it, know you'll use it, or feel you will.
Notes, files, and documents	They're old, outdated, and uninformative; they've been transferred to disk; or they no longer cover your derriere.	It's your duty to retain them, you refer to them often, or they have future value.
Reports and magazines	They're old, outdated, stacking up; you think you need them to keep up; or you fear a quiz on them.	They're vital to your career or well-being, you choose to retain them, or there *will* be a quiz on them.

Items	Toss or Recycle If ...	Retain If ...
Books, guides, and directories	You've copied, scanned, or made notes on the key pages; they're obsolete; or there is an updated version.	They're part of a life collection, you refer to them monthly, they have sentimental value, or you want them.
CDs, cassettes, and videos	You never play them, and if you do, they don't evoke any feelings or memories. They play poorly.	You play them, you like them, and you couldn't bear to part with them. They're a keepsake.
Outdated office equipment	You know who would like it as a donation, you can sell it, it's collecting dust, or it's in the way.	It serves a specific purpose, it adds to the decor, or it can be overhauled or revitalized.
Mementos and memorabilia	They no longer hold meaning, you have many similar items, you do not have room, or you've changed.	They still evoke strong memories, you will hand them down someday, or they look good on display.
Gifts, cards, and presents	They're never in use and are unwanted, and the giver won't know or be concerned that you tossed them.	You use them often, are glad you have them, or are saving them for some special reason.

THE 30-SECOND RECAP

- Every minute, more information is generated on Earth than you can possibly absorb in the rest of your life. There is no chance of keeping up with all the information. Fortunately, you can make choices about what to give your time and attention.

- Use prereaders to help you dramatically reduce the volume of information/reading that you face.

- Whittle out that which you do not need to retain both in your physical spaces and on your computer.

- For each item that you are retaining, use the chart at the end of the previous section to make a simple determination about whether the item is worth retaining or can easily be tossed.

LESSON 8
Taming Technology

In this lesson, you will learn how to manage voice mail, e-mail, facsimiles, and other high-tech equipment so that they will save you time rather than consume it.

YOU'VE GOT THE WHOLE WORLD IN YOUR PALM

For the foreseeable future, Moore's Law, which says that microchip capacity will double every 18 months, will continue unabated. That means that desktop computers will have awesome power, notebook computers will get thinner and be more versatile than ever, and palmtop computers are likely to become as universal as carrying a wallet. As of this writing, handheld computing devices or palmtops are already providing wireless links to the Internet, e-mail, and fax capabilities to users around the globe. Palmtops can store thousands of addresses, years' and years' worth of appointments, thousands of memos, and thousands of to-do items, all uniquely arranged based on user preferences.

PLAIN ENGLISH

Personal Digital Assistants (PDA) Another name for handheld computing devices or palmtops.

What else do these miniature wonders provide? They have the following capabilities:

- Support for a variety of software applications

- Automatic linking to a variety of hardware devices, peripherals, and accessories

- Quick access to information

- Battery life exceeding five hours

- Ultraconvenient, ultrapowerful address books, to-do lists, memo pads, calendars, trip logs, and expense calculators

- Enhanced, full-color, high-clarity screens

When choosing a palmtop device, you have various options:

- **Power:** Some palmtops use AA cells, AAA cells, or rechargeable lithium ion batteries.

- **Memory:** Anything from 2 megabits to 16 megabits is currently available, but this amount will change in a hurry. Some devices enable you to upgrade memory so that you can store more information.

- **Displays:** Palmtops are available in monochrome, four-level gray scale, 256 color, or 65,536 colors!

- **Screens:** Flip-up screens, back lighting, and high-color screens are some of the available options.

- **Other options:** Voice recognition, stereo headphones, bundled software, built-in modems, and flip-up screen covers are also available.

Even if you are not currently using a handheld computing device, the odds are astronomical that within a few short years you will be. Soon enough, the computing power on your wrist will exceed what was possible on a desktop in the 1990s. Regardless of the device you ultimately use, there are a variety of techniques that you can quickly and easily employ to ensure that you maximize your use of time when engaging in such functions as voice mail, e-mail, surfing the Internet, and faxing.

VOICE MAIL

You call another party, and you are subjected to the usual voice mail runaround: Press one for this; press two for that. After you finally find your way through the system, how do you leave a message that is succinct, has impact, and generates results? Unlike the old answering machines where you had to finish your message in 1 or 2 minutes, most systems today have no time limit. Yet it is to your benefit to finish in 45 seconds or less. Why? Attention spans are becoming shorter all the time, and people often become frustrated when they retrieve a 2- or 3-minute message.

 TIP

> The party you are trying to reach may have dozens of messages, so yours needs to be brief and elicit the type of response you want. (Lesson 9, "Keeping Interruptions to a Minimum," gives hints for leaving messages).

The biggest bugaboo of most people retrieving their voice mail is the speed at which people leave their telephone numbers. Because you know your number quite well, it's easy to say it so fast that the recipient must replay the part of the message with your phone number four or five times to get the whole number. A good rule of thumb is to say your number at the speed at which you can write it yourself, either on paper or with a finger in the air.

E-MAIL

With popular programs such as Outlook and Outlook Express, Netscape Communicator, Eudora Pro, and Claris, you have more than enough choices for e-mail software. Each program offers an impressive array of benefits and features.

Because all are downloadable, at least on a trial basis, and none is too difficult to learn, you could spend three or four days working with each one to gain a better understanding of what each provides. A faster and easier way would be to have co-workers or friends who already use one of the various programs as their e-mail mainstay walk you through the basic functions and let them allow you to do some test driving.

In terms of deftly handling e-mail, management trainer Laura Stack advocates a "6-D" system to handle e-mail regardless of what package you use:

1. **Discard it.** Delete the e-mail as soon as you receive it.

2. **Delegate it.** Forward it to someone else who can take care of it.

3. **Do it.** Respond to the e-mail, and then delete it.

4. **Dungeon it.** File it so that you can retrieve it again if you need to.

5. **Don't see it again.** Call the sender and get off the routing list.

6. **Decide.** When are you going to deal with it?

Notice that the 6-D system is related to the four-part system for handling paper files: Act on it, delegate it, file it, or recycle it.

CAUTION

> Some people print each e-mail that they can't handle immediately. Stack says that this will probably add to your office clutter, but if you have an organized way of handling these messages, go ahead and print them.

Unless you're waiting for some crucial message, it's best to check your mail about twice a day, and perhaps a third time if you're feeling ahead of the game. Some people become obsessed with checking their e-mail at every spare moment. These people usually spend too much time at work sending off letters to friends, passing on unsubstantiated virus warnings, and sending and receiving the latest jokes.

THE VERSATILE FAX MACHINE

With the advent of e-mail, the fax machine seems to have declined in status. Yet creative use of the fax machine in both sending and receiving can yield tremendous productivity and time-saving benefits. For example, instead of spelling out a five-line message to a distracted receptionist or having to slowly and carefully speak to a voice mail system, fax your information or request to others. Because all of your identifying information undoubtedly is already included on the fax form, you've saved a heap of time.

TIP

The best way of figuring out what combination of fax features is right for you is to find others who will walk you through the software they use and let you get a feel for the different systems.

Suppose you're trying to reach someone by phone, and despite using automatic redial, you're having trouble. Send a quick message by fax saying that you're having trouble getting through or listing the hours when you will be available to talk. Such a transmission accomplishes several objectives. You get your message through to the party you have been trying to reach, your phone line remains open to make or receive other calls, and the option is always available to include additional information on your fax transmission.

Depending on the type of phone service you have, long-distance phone and fax rates may be lower after 5 P.M. and before 8 A.M. Many commercial offices and home-based entrepreneurs have dedicated fax lines or fax lines that share limited online time. Because in many offices a gatekeeper (receptionist) or office early birds often arrive before 8 A.M., you can inexpensively submit a fax message to be forwarded to your target. The same holds true even if the office is closed.

As with e-mail, a variety of high-powered fax software programs are available with such features as multiple mailboxes, broadcast faxing, delayed transmission, enormous storage, speed dialing, alternative headers, custom cover pages, and extravagant reports. As the typical personal computer becomes more powerful, with more hard drive space, faster transmission speeds, more memory, and so on, the paper-handling aspects of faxing will noticeably diminish. More and more people will be able to receive your faxes and store them directly on their hard drives.

THE INTERNET PREVAILS

With 62 million Web sites now accessible and user-friendly applications becoming available all the time, the Internet is poised to take over as the dominant entertainment, communication, and information vehicle in society. It also can become a major time drain. Searching for the precise information you seek can tie up as much as 5 hours a week.

PLAIN ENGLISH

Bots   Software enabling you to automatically extract and receive information gathered from the Web based on your parameters or specifications.

Fortunately, on the heels of each problem related to using the Internet comes application software and service-oriented sites that provide an antidote. Because the specifics of the Internet change so quickly, I'll just describe broad-based categories of this type of help:

- **Bots:** The most popular bot is used for shopping. You can unload one of these little buggers, and it will search the

Internet all day long, giving you the best possible prices and best deals for the products and services you're seeking. Bots can also be used to ferret out information on health, travel, and on other bots!

- **Push software:** This software visits sites and topic areas that you preprogram to provide you with regular updated information from destinations on the Web that you deem important.

- **Mega search engines:** These search engines enable you to type a keyword or key phrase and automatically have an intelligent search of the top search engines. For example, www.google.com provides rosters of Web sites based on the number of links to particular site as opposed to what the sites' meta words and meta tags happen to say.

CAUTION

Meta words and meta tags can be artificially loaded with terms that have nothing to do with the site or that don't accurately reflect the information provided at the site.

- **Electronic clipping services:** Sites such as www.luceonline.com and www.cyberclipping.com offer you highly customized topic searches for a fee. For any single day, such sites can generate nearly everything that appears on the entire Web about a given company or topic.

Beyond employing application software and intelligent search engines to help you make better use of the Web, you can discover key sites that you might not otherwise have found by asking peers, clients, customers, or Web specialists which sites they have found helpful.

In general, good Web sites have these common features:

- **They keep visitors from getting lost.** A good Web site includes multiple links that take you back to the home page, to the previous page, or to another value-packed page of your choice. This type of navigation system ensures that you can quickly return to something familiar and comfortable or move forward to something else.

- **They go easy on the graphics.** Many Web sites are truly works of art by master graphic artists. However, smaller graphics and text-only hyperlinks, enable you to navigate much faster.

- **They include multiple contact links.** Good sites contain clear links that point you to contact information such as e-mail, fax, mail address, and phone numbers.

- **They are visitor-focused.** A good site focuses on your needs, ensuring that the most valuable information has the most direct access with the fewest graphics.

Sites that offer most of what is discussed here help you to optimize your time online.

GO FOR A WALK IN THE WOODS

As the world in general and your life in particular becomes ever more dependent upon communication technology supplying you with just in time information, education, and entertainment, it becomes that much more important to get away from this technology periodically. No virtual reality device, at least in the foreseeable future, will provide a quick substitute for all the sensations, physical exercise, and effect on your psyche of taking a walk in the woods, doing the backstroke in a tranquil lake, or skating through the park.

If the late twentieth century taught us anything, it was that although technology may increase the frequency of communication between parties at a distance, it doesn't necessarily promote or encourage in-depth relationships:

- It has not brought families closer together.

- It has not helped to decrease the rate of divorce in society.

- It has not conclusively resulted in increased scores on standardized tests among schoolchildren.

Use voice mail, e-mail, fax machines, the Internet, palmtops, and all manner of gadgetry to enhance your career, broaden your perspectives, and enrich your life. But withdraw from technology on a daily and regular basis in order to keep things in perspective. Remember that technology is a tool to help you accomplish goals that support your chosen priorities. Do not become a slave to technology, and do not allow the time you invest in technology to rob you of other vital aspects and experiences of a well-rounded life.

The 30-Second Recap

- When leaving a message on someone's voice mail, aim for 45 seconds or so and be clear, concise, and memorable. Leave your phone number at a speed at which it can easily be retrieved. Be upbeat, positive, and end succinctly.

- To gain a fuller understanding of the options available via e-mail and fax software, enlist others to give you a friend-to-friend demonstration. Get them to let you test-drive the software yourself so you can gain a first-hand experience as to what suits you and what does not.

- Use technology to enhance your career or life. Withdraw from it regularly to maintain perspective and to engage in experience that leads to a more balanced life.

LESSON 9

Keeping Interruptions to a Minimum

In this lesson, you'll learn how to reduce distractions, interruptions from others, and self-interruptions so that you can increase your concentration and improve your productivity.

HAVE YOU BEEN DISTRACTED TODAY?

It's far too easy to be distracted today: There is more competing for your time and attention now than at any time in history. By some estimates, world information is doubling every 68 days. More than 2,000 books are published worldwide every 24 hours, and more than 2,000 Web sites go online in the same period of time.

A study by the Reuters Group found that 33 percent of managers in industrialized nations are suffering ill health as a direct result of information overload. Nearly two thirds of these managers reported that they felt tension with colleagues and reduced job satisfaction and felt that it was directly related to the stress of information overload. Almost an equal number responded that their social and personal relationships have suffered as a result of the stress of having to cope with too much information. Chances are your responses would be much the same.

Staying in control of your time requires greater effort and vigilance than ever before. Fortunately, once you put a few simple practices into motion and stick to them, you'll find that it's entirely possible to carve out blocks of time for yourself.

GET SERIOUS ABOUT QUIET TIME

The ease with which you can visit any one of 62 million Web sites is the all-time potential distraction within the workplace. As recently as the early 1990s, surfing the Web at work wasn't a possibility for most people. Now, with a click of the mouse, you can go on the Internet and be exposed to more information than you could possibly digest.

With a simple effort, you can gain access to almost any information, organization, or person. And almost anyone can get in touch with you. People knock at your door, buzz you over the intercom, leave you voice mail, send you e-mail, page you, fax you, hand you memos, and mail things to you. Because distractions come in more forms than ever before, you need to be vigilant about barring yourself from them.

Although there might be more potential items competing for your time and attention at any given moment than any career professional of any previous generation could possibly have conceived of, the elements of maintaining focus and concentration remain the same:

- **Shut out all noise.** Forget what you read about having back-ground music playing while you're engaging in challenging tasks. Yes, background music has been proven to be effective for certain types of workers engaging in certain types of tasks, but engaging in any type of breakthrough or conceptual thinking requires your utmost concentration. Any competing noise in your environment potentially disrupts your ability to concentrate.

CAUTION

> Most workplaces are not completely free of noise, but don't let machine noises and HVAC sounds serve as an excuse as to why you can't offer your full attention to the task at hand.

- **Assemble the resources you need in advance.** This will diminish your need to get up and walk around to collect things. At the outset, the more prepared you are to tackle a project, the greater your chance of sticking with it.

- **Enlist the support of others.** If you're in an office environment, hang a sign on your door, circulate a memo, or broadcast an e-mail message that says essentially, "I need quiet from 9 to 11 this morning," or whatever timeframe suits you. Your co-workers may surprise you as to the level of support they offer you (that is, not bugging you during this time). After all, many of them seek the same thing you do.

- **Commit to the task at hand.** Unfortunately, many of us have been trained since an early age to divert our attention all over creation. We watch television shows where the typical camera angle changes every 3 to 5 seconds. We watch rock music videos where scenes shift in a second or less. All around us contemporary society seems to be telling us to give our attention everywhere all at once. Yet some of the tasks you face require several minutes of focused concentration, and some of them require several hours.

CAUTION

Unless you commit your mind and emotions to the task at hand, you're likely to find your concentration foundering.

- **Clear your desk and office** (see Lesson 6, "Managing Your Desk and Office"). Remove from view everything except what you need to work on the task at hand. The more items that visually compete for your time and attention, the more potential there is for you to be distracted. This is why it's often highly effective to work in the conference room, at a library table, or wherever else you have few items or materials to distract you.

KNOW THY TURF

The longer you've been working within an environment, the better able you are to pinpoint potential distractions at the outset. If you've been with your present organization for several years, then you're familiar with the office and building noises, when deliveries are made, when service professionals make their calls, and so forth. When you need to tackle that big, important project and you need as few distractions as possible, devote some effort at the outset to head off distractions.

Schedule your work to coincide with those times of least distractions. Also, flip off the ringer on your phone, tell your receptionist to hold all your calls until such and such a time, and announce at a group meeting that you'll be requiring quiet time on Thursday morning. In other words, pull out the stops to ensure that anticipated distractions are eliminated or at least diminished. Then, you'll have merely to deal with the unanticipated distractions, the likes of which I can't even begin to address in one short chapter.

INTERRUPTIONS FROM OTHERS

The larger the company or organization is, the greater the potential is for being interrupted by others. However, that doesn't mean that if you work in a small organization or business with a staff of only three, interruptions from others won't be a problem with you.

CAUTION

If you're working on something important, even one other person interrupting you at the wrong time or one too many times can throw you off course.

A study conducted by *Industrial Engineer*, a professional magazine, indicated that the average interruption sustained by a manager was only 6 to 9 minutes. Amazingly, the study also revealed that the average time it took such managers to recover from such interruptions was anywhere from 3 to 23 minutes.

So if the average interruption is 6 to 9 minutes with a midpoint of 7.5 minutes, and the average recovery time is 3 to 23 minutes, with a midpoint of 13 minutes, that means that the typical interruption results in 20.5 minutes of lost work. That being the case, it takes only one or two interruptions to nearly consume an entire hour. It takes only a few more interruptions a day to throw your entire schedule out of whack!

It's no surprise that interruptions prove to be the most stressful aspects of many people's jobs. A survey by the American Management Society reveals that 65 percent of the managers surveyed regard their jobs as more stressful than the average job. When asked to rank 15 workplace stressors, including workload, firing someone, working within budgets, balancing work and personal life, reprimanding or disciplining someone, and interruptions, the managers ranked interruptions as the most stressful of all!

CAUTION

If you don't try to minimize interruptions, you run the risk of getting far less done in a day than you had hoped for, feeling highly stressed, and having to face the same problem again and again.

Here are some ideas for keeping interruptions from others to the bare minimum:

- Devise a system where only a fraction of the questions that your staff has for you have to be asked of you. How can this be done? Any question that can be answered by asking a fellow staff member instead of you should be asked of that fellow staff member. Likewise, any question that could be answered by consulting the policies and procedures manual or department, division, or team memos should be consulted so that you don't need to field the question and incur the interruption.

- Any question that you need to answer that requires only a short answer should be asked of you in the least intrusive way. If the staff person can ask it by e-mail, have it asked by e-mail; if it can't wait, have them buzz you on the intercom, leave a voice mail message, or page you. Every time the question can be delayed have it be delayed until you're finished with the task at hand that demands your full concentration. When can a staff person interrupt you without trepidation? When the issue absolutely needs to be answered by you because it's big, it's important, and you wouldn't have it any other way.

TIP

Stratifying the types of interruptions that staff members make will cause the number of interruptions per person per week to fall dramatically, perhaps by as much as 75 percent.

- Prepare your staff as well as you can so that the answers to what they need to know can be readily found. Perhaps you can produce your own orientation kit, dossier, or briefing guide. Perhaps there's a set of Frequently Asked Questions (FAQs) worth preparing. Perhaps you can steer them toward your organization's intranet where such answers are provided. Perhaps there is a forum within the intranet where staff members exchange ideas.

- Tap one of your more senior staff members to be the surrogate manager during the time when you need quiet. As you'll see in Lesson 10, "Multiplying Your Time Through Delegation," the more often you can delegate tasks and responsibilities to others, the more your time is freed up. A good senior staffer should be able to deflect many of the questions and concerns that would otherwise come your way. The byproduct of handling this responsibility is that he or she one day will be able to handle the reins of manager. By that time, you'll have moved up as well.

- Give your good staff members multiple assignments (see Lesson 10) so that if they run into a road block on one, they can turn to something else instead of interrupting you during this time.

- Give staff members who have a propensity to ask many questions assignments that are relatively straightforward or routine for them. Then, for at least the duration of when you need a quiet, uninterrupted stretch, you'll know that they're tackling assignments that pretty much don't require your input.

INTERRUPTIONS IN THE AGE OF BEEPERS

Are you among the legions of professionals who have to wear a beeper as part of their overall responsibilities? If so, establish some simple protocols so that you can minimize the interruptions as a result of having to be on call.

Negotiate for some days during the week and some hours during specific days for which you will not have to be on call. In other words, you can turn off the beeper. As professionally and succinctly as possible, let your boss know that having to maintain constant responsiveness in the form of having to wear a pager greatly diminishes your ability to handle tasks and projects that call for deep concentration or highly creative thinking. A wise boss knows that this is true and is likely to grant you some beeper-free periods during the week as you requested.

CAUTION

When you can't work, go to lunch, take a nap, or even go to the restroom free of a pager or a cell phone, you're not really free to work and to live.

If you manage your own business or are otherwise in charge of when you wear a pager, recognize that you need stretches throughout the day and week when you won't be interrupted. If you're convinced of the need to be connected at all times, then chances are you're micromanaging, or overmanaging, all aspects of your business or your department, division, or staff. Micromanaging isn't pretty. In the short run, in a specific campaign, and during crunch time, it's okay. In the long run, it will keep you from rising to greater heights within your organization or within your own business.

NOT ALL MESSAGES ARE CREATED EQUAL

Another essential strategy, which I laid out in my book, *The Complete Idiot's Guide To Managing Your Time,* is to create a message hierarchy. Suppose that many of your cell phone calls and pages originate from a main source, such as an executive assistant. Work with that person and let him or her know when it is okay to interrupt you versus when it's best to hold messages until later, based on the following four-level system for deflecting pages:

Level A: Contact me now. This level includes messages that you want to receive, the sooner the better.

Level B: Contact me within X number of hours. This level includes messages about items that are important but not necessarily urgent (see Lesson 3, "Avoiding the Tyranny of the Urgent").

Level C: Contact me sometime later today. This level includes messages that you could receive at any time during the day because they're not time-related in the least. Fortunately, most messages fall into this category. When your assistant recognizes this, you'll gain more uninterrupted time, more often.

Level D: No need to contact me at all. This level includes messages or questions that your assistant might have felt were worth sending you in the past. Now, however, based on a clearer and mutual understanding of what needs to be transmitted and what doesn't, these messages no longer come to you because the assistant has the resources to find the answers to most questions and knows which messages you need to receive.

To make this system work, lavishly praise your assistant anytime he or she sends you a Level A message. Admonish the assistant anytime he or she sends a Level D message, because you never needed to be interrupted with that in the first place. Point out that, "That was a Level D message," if you happen to receive one.

Within a week, possibly even days, your assistant will be on the same wavelength as you and begin to understand what needs to be transmitted and when. This meeting of the minds will enable you to have uninterrupted stretches when you can do the things that you need to do.

EXTENDING THE PRINCIPLE

To avoid being interrupted by nonurgent phone calls, leave instructive messages on your voice mail and other answering devices that tell callers how their issues can be resolved. Announce in your messages that such and such person can take care of particular issues, or that you'll be available by phone Wednesday morning at 11:30, or that the best way to handle a particular problem is to e-mail the production department. In essence, deflect and win. If you have various voice mail boxes available, let callers know that they can gain the answer to questions about XYZ by pressing 1, pressing 2 will divert them to Sandra who can help them, and so on.

 TIP

> The more you're able to deflect and reroute messages to a person who can answer questions for you, the more uninterrupted time you'll have.

INTERRUPTIONS ARE MY BUSINESS

Suppose where you work constant interruptions are the norm, and you've been hired to take care of them. How can you remain effective, practice good time management, and still keep your sanity?

 TIP

> However deftly you dart from task to task, you'll do your best work if you concentrate on the task at hand, even if it's just for a brief time.

Think about when you're about to board a flight and then you hear an announcement that the flight has been canceled. Passengers in the airport lobby are up in arms. They rush to the gate agent and demand to be rebooked on the next flight immediately.

Does the gate agent handle 5 or 10 customers at a time? No. He or she focuses intently on the passenger who is first in line, eyeing the computer monitor to determine what alternatives are possible. The attendant works on that customer's new itinerary until it is complete. The process may take 3 minutes or 10 minutes. The skilled gate agent knows that there's no faster way to handle this mini-crisis than to stay calm and remain in control of the situation and to give full attention to the customer at hand.

Likewise, for every demand you face, eliminating distractions, reducing interruptions, and giving your full and undivided attention to the current task so that you can concentrate and do your best work is the best way to proceed.

THE 30-SECOND RECAP

- We live in an age that offers more distractions than anyone has ever faced previously. Thus, we must make a concerted effort to keep distractions to a minimum.

- The typical interruption at work is only 6 to 9 minutes. Recovery from the interruption, averaging 13 minutes, is what spells trouble. It only takes one interruption an hour to throw off your whole day.

- If you wear a pager, you have some special challenges to face because you're on call every minute of every hour of every day, theoretically. Strive to safeguard stretches of your time by working with others who are most likely to interrupt you. Also work with your boss so that you have some pager-free time throughout the week.

Lesson 10
Multiplying Your Time Through Delegation

In this lesson, you'll learn the do's, don'ts, principles, and techniques for delegation, as well as how to handle delegated responsibility.

Making It Work

It is said that management is the art of getting things done through other people. The most effective managers are skilled at delegating tasks and assignments to others and assuring that those assignments are successfully completed. Delegating is important to your career because the amount of time you can save by delegating is enormous.

TIP

> Nothing you do on your own can rival what you can do when you successfully harness the skills and ideas of others.

Before you delegate a task to somebody else, you have to know a little about that person:

- What is his or her workload?

- What are his or her skills?

- What kind of supervision is needed?

- How often do you need to follow up with this person?

You may be thinking, "This is a lot of information to have prior to delegating to somebody. If I have an assignment, can't I just hand it off?" You can, but the results are likely to be less than desirable. By understanding as much as you can about those to whom you delegate, you have the highest chance of delegating effectively and accomplishing your objectives.

Take the case of someone who reports to two bosses or more. If you're trying to delegate to such a person, you need to understand this person's workload. Perhaps he or she can share his or her assignment list or scheduling calendar with you. The more heavily burdened the worker is, the more important it is for you to schedule your task so as to fit the other person's schedule.

 TIP

> It's best to assign tasks that fit the interests, skills, and experiences of the worker. After all, you don't want somebody translating Greek, if they don't know one word of the language.

If you've worked with a person before, then you might have a reasonably good understanding of his or her working habits. Does this person need to check in with you regularly to ask several questions or receive your feedback and praise? Or is this person a self-starter who wants to receive primary instructions and then be allowed free reign in getting the job done?

 TIP

> The longer and more involved the task, the more often you'll need to check in with the worker. However, if it's something he or she has done before, oodles of instruction and follow-up may not be necessary.

THE DO'S OF DELEGATING

This list of quick do's will help make your delegating efforts more successful:

- **Do plan your delegations carefully before making them.** You want to parcel out doable assignments that are a reasonable match for the worker handling them.

- **Do offer clear instructions.** These instructions could be typed up, sent by e-mail, or perhaps recorded on cassette tape or videotape. Don't underestimate the value of taping your conversation when you make the assignment. Particularly if the assignment is something the worker has not done before or if the assignment is long and involved with many subparts, taping the session can have extreme benefit because the worker can play the tape and capture your exact words on an as-needed basis.

- **Do be flexible regarding the due date.** At times, you may have no alternative but to offer a fixed deadline. For many tasks, however, it may not make a difference to you exactly when the worker finishes the task.

 TIP

> When time is not critical, offer a due date to the worker and then be generous when he or she misses by a day or two.

- **Do ensure that the worker has sufficient resources to get the job done.** There is nothing worse than assigning people to your project and then watching them fail because they don't have the right equipment, staff, or other resources at their disposal. In your role as delegator, work with staff to ensure that they know sufficient support is available.

- **Do monitor progress as is practical.** Be available for questions and guidance. Ideally, the worker takes the project, doesn't bug you for a single second, and returns with everything done correctly and on time. Realistically, the worker is going to need to get back in touch with you on occasion for questions, concerns, and sometimes just to have a sounding board. If you recognize this in advance, you have a better chance at being effective.

- **Do be both firm and flexible.** Convey an accurate picture of what needs to be done, but allow leeway in how it's accomplished. Sometimes the worker will approach a problem in an entirely different way than you would. That's okay if it gets the job done, if it doesn't tie up an inordinate amount of resources, and if the work is delivered on time.

TIP

> Pay attention to how workers complete projects. Often, you'll get wind of some new procedure that's faster and more effective than how you would have done the job yourself.

- **Do acknowledge the worker's contributions.** Everyone likes recognition for his or her efforts. You, of course, are more interested in results. Because sufficient efforts lead to results, you increase the probability of having the end result being what you want by acknowledging efforts throughout the process. Offer constructive feedback when you sense or see that the project is heading somewhat off course.

- **Do keep records of how the project was completed.** When the job is completed, make notes as to what the worker completed, the skills and ingenuity he exhibited, and other observations about accomplishment of the task. Later, you can draw upon these notes in devising more assignments to be delegated.

DELEGATION TAKES TIME

Undoubtedly you have heard the expression, "If you want to get something done, do it yourself." This expression was probably coined by someone who was not an effective delegator.

Yes, there are some tasks you could finish yourself in the time it takes you to explain what needs to be done to someone else. If the task is not recurring, go ahead and do it yourself. However, for any other type of task, it pays for you to explain to someone what you want done. Taking the time to explain a task helps establish a system in which this particular task or others like it no longer need to stay on your plate; you're training somebody else how to relieve your burden.

CAUTION

If it's taking longer to explain how to do something than it would take to do it on your own, keep in mind that your efforts will bear fruit the next time the task is delegated.

Anytime two or more parties are working together, however, the probability for unsuccessful results is present. Much of what is delegated is not handled properly or is not turned in on time. Why? Sometimes the task was not delegated to the right person. More often than not, however, the way in which the task was delegated was insufficient.

THE DON'TS OF DELEGATION

Avoid these pitfalls when delegating a task to another person:

- **Don't rush.** Don't be in such a rush to hand the assignment over to someone else that you do not fully explain all the steps involved to successfully complete the project.

- **Don't pass on incomplete instructions.** If you give the worker a list of instructions, make sure the instructions are complete. Leaving out one little thing that seems obvious to you may spell the worker's downfall.

- **Don't ignore the worker's concerns.** Delegating involves a lot of explaining, but it also involves a lot of listening. Be prepared to listen to the questions and concerns of the worker. Listen between the lines for the worker's fears.

TIP

> Receiving a new task can be a little scary for a worker. Also, depending on how much else competes for his time and attention, the worker may feel stressed or anxious.

- **Don't give the wrong image of yourself.** Don't profess to be open to questions and concerns and then make yourself unavailable. A little frustration for the workers can turn into a major one if you're not around to handle the 10-second question that would get them back on the right path. (Think about how you feel when you're trying to learn a new software package. Would you rather spend a half hour trying to find the right keystroke combination to proceed or ask somebody who can show you in 10 seconds?)

- **Don't arbitrarily delegate to anyone.** Pick a person for the job who can schedule the task, handle it effectively, and turn it in on time.

- **Don't think your way is the only way.** Don't be so concerned if the worker proceeds differently than you would, as long as the worker is progressing toward the desired result. Offer sufficient slack for the worker to get the job done in the way he or she sees fit, as long as he or she is not unnecessarily expending resources and taking inordinate amounts of time.

WHAT TO DELEGATE

Often, otherwise effective career professionals don't make the progress in their careers that they otherwise could because they are not delegating enough to others. The more competent one is, the more often one is likely to keep too many tasks on one's own to-do list. Therefore, examine all the tasks and projects on your plate with an eye as to where you can get help.

CAUTION

> As a manager, you want to cultivate your ability to work with and through other people, as opposed to continuing to take on more and more on your own.

Suppose you're a sales manager who is working later and later into the evening and enjoying it less. Even the most junior staff person within your office can give you enormous help, if you expand your view of what can be delegated. For example, with a little time and effort, this junior person could be put in charge of handling customer requests for information by directing people to the Web site, mailing out literature, and referring people to the appropriate party within your department.

What other kinds of tasks could be delegated to even the most junior person on your staff? Here are some ideas:

- Sending out mailings of any sort. If you have a flyer or a brochure that needs to go out to targeted recipients, initiating this campaign and handing it over to a junior staff person makes good sense.

- Routing and sorting incoming mail.

- Serving routine customer needs. This person could establish a list of FAQs (frequently asked questions).

- Producing a department or division directory of key staff and how to reach them and offering customers contact information, product announcements, and service literature.

- Picking up and delivering things.

- Researching or surveying customers to learn more about their needs and potential opportunities for additional sales. Research could be as simple as gathering articles on the customer base or visiting some customer sites and making notes. Surveys could be as brief as five questions asked over the phone, via e-mail, via fax, or simple mail campaign.

- Keeping track of trade publications. This person could set up a small library that also houses key directories and industry newsletters.

- Logging names into the customer database. Whether you use Access, ACT!, GoldMine, or any of the other popular databases, virtually anyone who has worked with a PC can be instructed how to enter names in as little as 5 minutes.

- Studying competitors' literature, products and services, Web sites, and publications. What better way to keep on top of what others are doing than by having the most junior staff person of your office assemble dossier packets for each of the sales professionals?

- Doing searches on the Web. If you want to find a particular product or service, company, or organization, make a list and hand it over. Your time will be freed up, you'll get the answers you'll need, and you'll feel more in control of your day.

- Tracking or arranging inventory or displays, setting up materials at trade shows, or shipping materials to and from trade shows.

- Proofreading or double-checking copy for marketing literature, memos, sales letters, follow-up letters, and boilerplate materials.

- Doing many other things that you don't need to be doing, because with a little instruction and a little guidance, this worker can handle your delegated assignments.

PLAIN ENGLISH

> **Mettle**   Value or worthiness, particularly when tested by challenging conditions.

After this worker has gained some experience as a result of all you have delegated, you can then delegate even more important tasks and free up more of your time. Here are some of the higher order tasks that you can delegate to workers as they prove their mettle:

- **Call customers after a sale to see whether they feel satisfied, what else they may need, and how they feel about the purchase.** This kind of follow-up is an excellent way to learn about your product or service performance, and you often gain critical feedback from customers that you ordinarily wouldn't have time to collect. Many companies are able to make quick follow-up sales as a result of these calls that they wouldn't ordinarily be able to make.

- **Seek out new sources of supply.** Depending on what you offer, the price of supplies and raw materials that you use may differ widely. A junior staff person can get on the Web and start making comparisons or go to industrial directories, such as Thomas's register, or even the yellow pages of your phonebook and make inquiries. Having someone periodically assess new sources of supply and delivery can make the difference between having a profitable quarter and having a highly profitable quarter.

DELEGATING TO HIGHLY EFFECTIVE WORKERS

If you're blessed to be working with a highly effective staff, you're likely to have rewarding experiences when it comes to delegation. You may have the opportunity to delegate often and even delegate several assignments at once. Effective workers understand their productive peaks and valleys throughout the course of a day and a normal week.

When you delegate several tasks to a good worker, he or she instinctively knows how to maintain high productivity by handling assignments on those days and at those hours that achieve a relatively constant effort-to-task ratio. Good workers know how to harness their varying energy levels throughout the workweek so that they know what can best be tackled when.

If you give such an employee several assignments and can be flexible as to when they're due, you'll receive each of the completed assignments in a manner that probably exceeds what you would have expected. Productive employees have their own internal time grid. Allowed to pace themselves, they can accomplish more and remain energetic.

 TIP

> Continually meeting with someone who offers arbitrary deadlines is draining. So when you give good employees assignments, let them work out the schedule.

Here are some additional tips to delegating to highly effective employees:

- Provide enough and varied assignments so that the worker knows what to undertake and when.

- Be as flexible as you can regarding when assignments are due. Good employees tend to finish the important jobs on time. They finish the less important assignments as soon as possible thereafter.

- Avoid late afternoon assignments and surprise assignments throughout the week. Sometimes this isn't possible because you've been hit with a surprise and have no choice but to pass it on. However, try not to upset the personal productivity cycle the good workers have already established for themselves in accordance to the assignments you have already delegated to them.

- Always seek to provide enough advance notice of assignments so that productive employees have sufficient time to integrate the new assignment into their current schedule of assignments.

DELEGATING TO VETERANS

When working with more senior workers, you have the opportunity to delegate large tasks and projects. In this case, it makes sense to build follow-up into the overall assignment period. Perhaps you meet every Thursday at 10 A.M., or perhaps you exchange e-mails at the end of each day. Or perhaps you have a Monday morning chalk talk, where you chart the progress of the project, make course corrections, see what additional resources are required, and so on.

TIP

> For larger, ongoing projects that you have delegated, your regular input becomes a vital resource in the overall success of the project.

Suppose you've delegated several large projects to several different veteran workers. You may end up having several meetings about these projects throughout the week. In each case, you are ensuring that the entrusted staff person stays on course in the critical projects you have delegated. That's just fine, and that's what a good manager does.

Ideally, everything on your plate would be handed off to others, and you would work in a supervisory capacity, guiding here, cajoling there, extending resources there, and so on. This is not to be confused with having people interrupt you all day and all week long (see Lesson 9, "Keeping Interruptions to a Minimum") for questions and concerns that you don't need to be exposed to.

As you rise within your organization, you may find that regular meetings with key staff or entire teams to whom you've delegated assignments becomes the norm. (See Lesson 13, "Streamlining Your Meetings," for advice on having more effective meetings.) That's fine; you're doing your job.

One day you may find yourself as CEO, where you're literally handing off everything, keeping your eye focused on the big picture of the organization, making critical decisions, and offering crucial observations and advice. Consider the president of the United States. He doesn't do anything, but rather relies on a bevy of top advisors, top administrators, and top White House staff to ensure that the wheels of the nation stay well oiled.

THE 30-SECOND RECAP

- Effective managers are effective delegators. The higher you want to rise in your organization, the more important it will be for you to delegate.

- You have considerable leeway when it comes to delegating tasks to good workers. You can give them several assignments, and if you're flexible with your due dates, they'll perform in a manner that meets or exceeds your expectations.

- Even the most junior person on your staff can handle a wide variety of assignments with a minimum of direction and support. The more often people handle tasks that are appropriate for them, the less guidance and fewer resources they require in order to be successful.

Lesson 11

Avoiding the Time Traps

In this lesson, you will learn how to say no without fear, defeat perfectionism, manage your anger, and avoid other time traps such as television and idle time.

The Fear of Saying No

You are requested to do something at work, and your automatic response is "Sure." You are asked to attend something that you would rather not attend, but you agree to go. Many career professionals who have little problem saying no in their home life find that saying no in the workplace is difficult. And this difficulty causes time management problems.

> **CAUTION**
>
> Simply uttering the word *no* is difficult for many people.

Suppose a co-worker asks you to participate in some extra-curricular activity after work. Suppose, too, that it is an activity you enjoy, but it is not something that you care to engage in right now. Your plate is already full. It makes far more sense for you to get home early at night than to hang around for yet another activity that consumes your precious leisure time.

Nevertheless, you want to be one of the pack, part of the in-crowd. So what do you do? You say, "Sure, why not?" Thereafter, every Tuesday you find yourself lingering at work for another hour, getting home later than you prefer, and resenting the fact that you agreed to be part of the group. Maybe it's the kind of a group where each meeting draws you in further. Perhaps you have some crucial responsibility. Everyone is counting on you. Now, you can't withdraw even though the time investment is upsetting you.

Let's look at a second scenario. You're invited to attend a one-time event. Perhaps it is a retirement party for Bob up on the third floor, or maybe you have been invited to attend a baby shower for Jessica in production. Maybe you have been asked to volunteer one Saturday two months from now, and it appears that your schedule is open. So you say yes to the retirement party, the baby shower, and the Saturday volunteer job.

When you stop and think about each activity, however, what you wanted to say was no. You've never liked Bob; you simply said hello to him a few times in the hall and tolerated his corny jokes. If you go, it would be for reasons of office politics, which have some value. As for Jessica, what is this, her third or fourth child? Didn't you attend a shower of hers two and a half years ago where you were utterly bored?

When you looked at your calendar two months in advance and saw that the time for the Saturday volunteer effort was wide open, it was relatively easy for you to say yes. When you have no competing responsibilities or scheduled items, why not be generous with your time? Yet a curious phenomenon occurs as you approach that date for which you said that you would volunteer. Your schedule starts to fill in, and when the date of your volunteering finally arrives, you barely have enough time to honor your commitment. Again you become resentful and wish you had said no two months before.

DECLINE WITH TACT AND EMPATHY

The common denominator in these situations is the inability to politely and tactfully decline an invitation. It's one thing if your boss asks you to take on extra work or your team is staying late one evening to tackle some tough problem that hasn't gone away after considerable effort. It is quite another issue to participate in all manner of quasi-office activities presented to you, largely as a function of your working in that environment.

Take the case of Bob's retirement party. Have you ever had lunch with Bob? Have you and he ever had a meaningful conversation of longer than 5 minutes? Has Bob helped you in some specific way, or have you helped Bob in some specific way? Do you share any kind of bond? If the answers to these questions are no, no, no, and no, why would you want to attend Bob's retirement party? For appearances? Perhaps. Out of respect? Possibly. Because you feel it is your duty? No way.

What could you say when presented with the invitation? Try these statements:

- "I wish Bob well, but I'm already committed for that time."

- "Please express my congratulations. Unfortunately, I'll be unable to attend."

- "I promised my son that we would XYZ, but give Bob my best."

- "I can't attend, but I would like to offer a small gift, what do you suggest?"

- "Sounds like it will be a great event, but that evening I'll be at XYZ."

In the case of the baby shower, similar responses will work, as well as the following: "Oh my, this will be my fourth shower in about four months. I'll have to pass on this one," or "I appreciate the invitation, but I'm already scheduled."

Finally, in the case of someone asking you to commit your time at some distant point, be on guard! As I relayed in *The Complete Idiot's Guide to Managing Your Time*, we all tend to fall into the trap of believing that two to three months from now our calendar or our schedule will somehow work itself out and the time pressure that we feel today will subside. The first step in helping your cause is to not say yes when you prefer to say no.

Here are some appropriate and tactful ways to decline requests for your time at some distant future date:

- "That's going to be too close to the time when our family is going to be traveling."

- "I can't make a commitment right now; I'll know better in a couple of weeks."

- "I appreciate the invitation, but Saturday afternoon is the time when I do XYZ."

- "It sounds worthwhile, but count me as doubtful. I need that time to XYZ."

TIP

When declining an offer, acknowledge the invitation and respect the fact that the event has importance to the inviter. Also convey your good wishes even if you can't attend.

You cannot give someone a flat-out no without explanation. They will be offended, have hurt feelings, or feel somehow that they have let you down or wronged you in the past and now you are retaliating.

Therefore, the no's that you offer need to be respectful and firm while being gracious and compassionate.

DEFEAT PERFECTIONISM

At times, the drive for perfectionism is appropriate. A doctor performing a complex operation, a pilot landing a jumbo jet plane, and a police detective investigating a murder all need to strive to do the best possible job. Yet even these professions have times and situations where perfectionism is unnecessary, unwarranted, and overly time consuming. For the doctor, a bandaging job that is 95 percent toward perfect is just fine. For the airline pilot, a landing where one wheel touches down a half second after the other does not diminish the quality of the flight. For the police detective, not interviewing an eleventh witness after interviewing 10 witnesses who independently corroborate each other's observations is probably okay.

In your own work, there are countless times throughout the day that not being perfect makes more sense from the standpoint of practicality and saving time than striving for perfection. When you're assembling data to make a decision, the opportunity before you may have passed if you wait to decide until you have reams of information. If you collect too much data, then you get to a point where you are more confused than informed. Assemble only the body of information necessary to help you feel comfortable with your decision, but no more than that. Let go of the tendency to overcollect.

TIP

Many decisions made based on instinct and intuition turn out just fine. This is because all the data to which you have ever been exposed is brought to bear when you're making a decision.

Look for opportunities throughout the workday where a 90 or 95 percent effort is just fine. If you're turning in a report, and your department is structured so that the production team does copyediting, it doesn't pay for you to turn in a 100 percent grammatically correct report. Studies show that the additional time that you spend to take a project from the 95 percent mark to the 100 percent mark is not worth it in most cases. Driving for perfection (that is, ensuring that the final 5 percent is done correctly) often takes as much time as the initial 95 percent effort required!

When giving instructions to your staff, if you give them 9 or 10 suggestions on how to effectively do a job, but forget one or two suggestions, your staff will still have plenty to work with. If you strive to give them every great suggestion you can come up with, the time and effort that you expend may be inordinate, and the marginal value of the extra suggestions for your staff may not be nearly worth the effort.

PLAIN ENGLISH

> **Environment**   One's surroundings; in the context of the workaday world, one's office and surrounding offices and, in general, one's workplace.

AVOID CREATING THE PERFECT ENVIRONMENT

Some people waste oodles of time trying to create the perfect environment before starting tasks. They adjust the blinds just so. They sharpen three pencils. They refill their cup of coffee. They wait until the top of the hour. They stack up the papers on their desk neatly.

To be sure, there is nothing wrong with arranging your immediate environment in accommodation with the way you work. Having your office and work setting the way you want it is conducive to your productivity. The problem starts when you find yourself continually in the need of having a perfect environment before getting anything done. Delaying the start of a project until everything is just right is just a form of procrastination.

MANAGE YOUR ANGER

What does managing your anger have to do with a lesson on avoiding time traps? Isn't it natural to get upset on occasion? Yes, it is. The problem with anger from a time standpoint is how long it takes you to overcome its effects so that you can get back to rational, clear-headed thinking.

Some people go into a tizzy over the smallest of things and spend half the morning stewing about it. If your anger has arisen, how can you mute its effects so as to not waste time and be rather ineffectual while you are in a state of anger? Here are some suggestions:

- Decide how much time you are going to allow yourself to be angry. A reasonable timeframe is 5 minutes. Then hold yourself to it. When the appointed time comes, get back to the job at hand.

- Pull out a motivation-inspiring poem, passage from a book, or a saying, particularly those passages that you have already earmarked as effective for getting you back on track during times when you are otherwise out of sorts.

- Talk to a co-worker or call a friend who is good at listening, can help you work things out, and can help you get back on track in near record time.

- Take that walk, count to 10, throw cold water on your face, or engage in any other activity rationally used to ward off anger.

The following suggestions can work just as well, after you have blown your top:

- **Fight for objectivity.** Try to look at the big picture. Take whatever incident occurred and keep it in context.

- **Write down how you are feeling and why.** Sometimes the mere act of expressing your thoughts on paper helps to release some of the pent-up emotion. Afterward, chuck the piece of paper.

- **Break your routine.** If your anger arose while you were sitting, then stand. If you were standing, then sit. If you were in motion, then stop. If you were inside, then go outside. If you were outside, then go inside. For many people, a change of venue improves their mood greatly.

- **Change your physiology.** If you throw your shoulders back, stand erect, and force a small smile, your psychology begins to follow. Studies have shown that people who hold their heads up high, smile, and walk proudly, feel more confident than people who mope along, stare at the ground, and let their shoulders droop. Likewise, it is hard to feel angry if your physiology emulates something other than the closed, clenched, restricted posture that is characteristic of anger.

PLAIN ENGLISH

> **Physiology**   The science that deals with processes and functions of living organisms.

- **Get physical.** I don't mean punch somebody. Rather, stretch, practice isometrics, or if no one is around, do jumping jacks. By getting physical, you divert your energy and focus from anger.

TURN OFF THE BOOB TUBE

Do you arrive at work exhausted some mornings? If so, there are probably identifiable behaviors that you engage in that lead to such a situation. You stay up a little late, watch an extra television show or two, and find yourself getting to bed a little later than your body needs. The simple truth in Western society, and increasingly throughout the world, is that too many of us watch too much television too often.

CAUTION

> Sitting and watching television zaps your creativity. Television's words, sounds, graphics, and images tend to drown out your imagination.

It's time to recognize television for what it is: a plug-in drug. Sure, there are dozens of worthwhile programs in the course of a week, including movies worth seeing, educational shows, and history programs. Sometimes the show is good: The themes are compelling, and you actually learn something. However, how often do you focus on these highly worthwhile programs? And even if you limited your focus to these programs, do you watch in measured amounts, maintaining a balance of other activities? Watching even the best television show pales by comparison with what you could learn by reading great literature, participating in your community, or being a parent, a spouse, or a friend to a live person.

CAUTION

> The average person spends nine solid years of his life watching how other people supposedly live on television.

Japan and other Southeast Asian cultures that now find themselves thoroughly ensconced in television programming have experienced the following marked, undesirable changes in their societies in the last decade:

- The attitude of workers has changed.
- Materialism runs rampant.
- People are awash in gadgets and electronic goods.

DISCOVER AUDITORY MEDICATION

Radio can instill the same languor as television. When you drive to work in the morning, do you turn on the radio to listen to some shock jock dispense his brand of socially contemptible humor? These shock jocks are paid megadollars to medicate you for 15 or 20 minutes while you make your way through roads jam-packed with cars.

What is the harm, you say, in listening to some witty, if not deviant, shock jock while making your way into work? After all, you have to be in the car anyway, so how can this be a drain on your time? The problem lies in the opportunity cost of what else you could be doing with your time in the car:

- Listening to classical music would filter into your being and prepare you from a physiologic standpoint to have a more pleasant morning.

- Listening to a book on tape or motivational tape could provide you with new insights while entertaining you and stimulating your imagination.

- If you share a ride on the way into work, conversing with a friend can yield many benefits.

If you find yourself automatically flipping on the television as soon as you get home or flipping on the radio as soon as you get in the car, and think that you are not hooked on these devices, then try this simple test. For one week, every time you get into your car, drive for at least 5 minutes before turning on the radio. If you're like most people, you'll probably find that you can't do it.

At home, go a whole evening without turning on the television. If you are able to do that (and you will be among the few), go a whole weekend without doing it. Likewise, rather than wantonly surf the Web, engage in something else for a weekday evening or weekend.

These activities are not simply exercises in abstinence, but rather they are telling indicators of just how much we have allowed the electronic connection to infiltrate our lives and, in many respects, dominate our lives.

CAUTION

> There are certainly good things to hear on the radio and many Web sites worth exploring. The problem arises when you allow such media to overstep its bounds and facilitate the ease with which you idle away your hours, your days, your weeks, and your life.

THE 30-SECOND RECAP

- Until you learn how to say no with grace and ease, you are likely to find yourself saying yes to all manner of activities that you prefer not to be involved in.

- Depending on your profession, there are situations in which it pays to do a perfect job. For most people, however, perfectionism is a huge time trap.

- Turning off your television may be the single most effective step you can make to reclaim your time.

LESSON 12
Managing Stress

In this lesson, you'll learn how to cope with stressful environments by modifying your type A behavior, avoiding common stressors, and adopting new techniques that reduce the impact of stress.

WATCH OUT FOR SIGNS OF STRESS

Unquestionably, the office environment of today is more stressful than it was a generation ago. Back then, people didn't have to cope with fax machines, e-mail, elaborate phone systems, pagers, the Internet and intranets, and all the other ways of communicating that exist today. A generation ago, there wasn't the same level of unrelenting global competition. Technological change, and change in general, didn't come at nearly as rapid a pace as it does today. Competition for your time and attention both in the workplace and at home was nothing like it is today.

Chances are, even if you work in a highly enlightened organization that has ergonomically designed your office and the office environments all around you, you nevertheless feel stress on a recurring basis.

PLAIN ENGLISH

> **Ergonomics**   The relationship between furniture, equipment, resources, and individuals engaged in using them.

Signs that you're experiencing stress abound. A few common indications are the following:

- Less abundant saliva, leaving your mouth and throat dry
- Jaw pain or pressure, indicating that you are clenching your teeth
- Short, shallow breathing
- Being more prone to colds and flus
- Headaches of all kinds
- Gas and heartburn
- Higher heart rate, resulting in an increase in blood pressure

Stress can also show up in more subtle ways:

Lack of concentration	Not trusting others
Frequent illness	Losing interest in sex
Insomnia	Heightened anxieties
Persistent fatigue	Becoming easily fatigued
Irritability	Increased use of alcohol and drugs
Nail biting	Feeling like life has no meaning
Hunger for sweets	Having no direction or purpose
Tending to minutia	Feeling shallow or uncharitable
Tardiness	Indigestion or irritable bowels
Absenteeism	Being chemically dependent
Combativeness	Pains in specific parts of the body
Unexplained depression	Irregular menstrual cycles
Nervous giggling	Tapping your feet
Wishing you could hide	Frequent trips to the bathroom
Having bad dreams	Resenting others

TAKE CHARGE AND WIN

The fastest and easiest way to diminish stress related to your immediate environment is to take charge. Go ahead and get whatever devices and office accoutrements will help you to work more blissfully.

If noise is an issue, try to get approval to install noise-dampening furniture. If your company will not pay for it, go to an office furniture store and walk the aisles. Are there inexpensive, light, sound-dampening partitions you can purchase? If not, perhaps you might find it useful to buy an electronic sound screen, such as Sound Screen by Marpac Corporation. The Sound Screen is a portable white noise device that emits different frequencies and amplitudes of a droning, nondisruptive blanket of sound. You can use this device to minimize the effects of startling or disruptive sounds outside your office. (For more information, contact Marpac Corporation at P.O. Box 3098, Wilmington, NC 28406-0098 or fax 919-763-4219.)

PLAIN ENGLISH

White noise   Frequencies and amplitudes of a droning, non-disruptive blanket of sound.

What else can you do to make your immediate environment more pleasant for you? Find out whether you're allowed to hang posters, bring in plants, or display pictures of loved ones. Ask whether you can modify the lighting, temperature, or ventilation of your workspace to better suit you. Even the smallest of changes can make a dramatic impact on your productivity.

Potential sources of workplace stress include the following:

Monotony	Being passed over
Noise	Missing an opportunity
Deadlines	Role ambiguity
People	Conflicting demands

Overwork	Lack of job security
Unrealistic expectations	Being underused
Uncertainty	Inflexible work environment
Lack of control	Lack of visible career progression
Emergency and crises	Firing someone
Being underappreciated	Repeatedly being given last-minute assignments

Fortunately, there are many techniques you can employ anytime throughout the workday when your head starts pounding, or your insides start shaking, or you feel like you're going to explode. Here's a brief list of options (excerpted from my book *The Complete Idiot's Guide to Managing Stress*):

1. **Maintain a sense of humor.** Laughing in the face of tough challenges can defuse stress, lower your blood pressure, and prevent you from losing your temper.

2. **Stretch regularly.** Shake out the kinks by standing tall and reaching for the ceiling. Or try circling your head or doing deep knee bends. Just remember to close the office door first.

TIP

All other things being equal, you're going to feel less stressed the better the shape you're in.

3. **Communicate with co-workers.** Find a good listener and talk to somebody, particularly a co-worker who has a sympathetic ear.

4. **Employ imaging.** By focusing on a positive image for even as little as a minute or two, you can achieve a drop in pulse, heart rate, and even blood pressure. For example, you might remember a meadow or farm from your childhood, a waterfall, a picnic site, a scene from a movie, a favorite cousin, or a lover.

5. **Avoid turning daily obstacles into catastrophes.** Daily roadblocks and setbacks are nearly guaranteed. Don't let them get the best of you.

6. **Get a massage.** A good masseuse can work your lymphatic system and help your body to flush out toxins that may have built up. You'll sleep like a baby that night.

7. **Take a walk.** A five-minute walk can make a world of difference. The key is to not be in a hurry.

TIP

Walk purposefully, stretching out your legs and swinging your arms as you go. Maintain your best posture. Take good deep breaths while you walk and notice your surroundings.

8. **Drink some water.** Keep a bottle of mountain spring water in your office or nearby. Your body needs to hydrate itself continuously. When you travel a lot, particularly when you fly, or you find yourself under stress, drinking water is a quick, reliable way to feel at least a little better.

TYPE A IS OKAY

Years ago, you may have read that if you're a type A personality, a hard-driving person who works long hours, you're likely to be more stressed than other people. Let the trumpets sound: This isn't necessarily true.

If you exhibit aggressive and hostile tendencies, type A behavior is harmful, but otherwise, a type A person's stress level is not likely to be higher than anyone else's. Some people are quite comfortable being type A's all the time. However, if you attempt to change your stripes and act like someone you're not, your stress level may increase.

Whether you're type A or type B, you're much more likely to avoid stress if you're operating the controls and levers of your career and life.

ADOPTING NEW TECHNIQUES

If your stress has been too strong or gone on for too long, you may be primed for trying the following proven, if involved, techniques for keeping your stress in check:

- **Guided imagery:** Guided imagery is like visualization except that another person takes you through a series of steps designed to bring you to a more relaxed state. The instructor or group leader may first ask you to close your eyes, sit erectly but comfortably, and perhaps concentrate on some part of your body or your breathing. The session may include progressive relaxation, which is a stress-reduction technique that involves repeatedly tensing each muscle of the body and then letting it go. If you try this on your own, you'll see that after the third time that you ease up, your muscles feel more relaxed, perhaps even warm.

- **Self-talk:** Does some 80 percent or more of your internal dialogue focus on your shortcomings? Most of what people say to themselves is negative:

  "I know that I could've done better, I'm always messing things up."

  "I'd like to meet that person over there, but I'll probably blow it."

  The key in making self-talk work for you, particularly in regards to reducing stress, is to be more conscious of what you say to yourself. Focus on making positive statements to yourself?

TIP

> Generate a list of positive statements that you can use and write them down or tape them on cassette. Such a list will help you to replace the negative statements that you routinely offer yourself.

- **Aromatherapy:** Some substances in nature help you to feel calm and serene. For some people, the smell of pine works wonders; for others, it's lemon. If you add oil of lavender to your next hot bath, your weary soul and fatigued body will receive a treat that many people never discover. Any health food or bath and beauty store should provide many aromas to choose from.

TIP

> Chlorophyll is another smell that helps many people reduce stress and feel more energetic. This is why so many people get energized in the spring. Instead of waiting for spring, try surrounding yourself at home and work with greenery.

- **Vitamins:** Vitamins can be a major factor in keeping stress in check. Vitamins B and C help to nourish the adrenal glands, which release stress hormones as your body prepares for fight, flight, or the long-term, low-level, insidious stress that is so prevalent today. Calcium and magnesium help to fortify your nervous system. Most multiple vitamins are worth taking, although depending on how much they cost, what doses of which vitamins are included, and what your specific needs are, one brand can be much better for you than another.

- **Deep breathing:** Deep, diaphragmatic breathing is an important stress reducer for everyone. Imagine that there is a balloon in your stomach. As you inhale, you fill up the balloon. As you exhale, you deflate the balloon. In both cases, there's no need to rush. The balloon can fill slowly and empty slowly. Your chest and shoulders do not need to be a part of the process (it's much better if they're not). As you achieve deep, diaphragmatic breaths, your chest and whole torso will move, but they are not actively involved in the process.

TIP

> To check that you are breathing diaphragmatically, lie on the floor. Breathe as you normally would while placing one or both hands over your stomach, near your navel. Do you feel that up-and-down motion? You're breathing diaphragmatically!

- **Meditation:** Meditation is a way of focusing on deeper thoughts and feelings by turning away from the distractions and tensions of everyday living. To meditate is to focus your mind while in a state of relaxed awareness. You're not asleep, and you are not in a trance. The goal of meditation is to free your mind from accumulated tension and to reach a divine emptiness from which deep concentration and relaxation are possible. If you meditate often, over time, you can get to the point where you don't respond so intensely to potential external stressors. Many people swear by meditation, citing it as the single best method for achieving an improved level of calmness and serenity.

THE 30-SECOND RECAP

- The fastest and easiest way to diminish stress related to your immediate environment is to take charge of your immediate environment.

- Simple techniques for alleviating stress include maintaining a sense of humor, talking to someone, employing imaging, avoiding turning minor problems into catastrophes, getting a massage, taking a walk, and drinking some water.

Lesson 13
Streamlining Your Meetings

In this lesson, you'll learn ways to start meetings on time, keep them on track, and reduce the overall meeting time while achieving the desired objectives.

Make the Most of Meetings

Despite the fears of some people years ago that in the future there would be fewer face-to-face meetings between real live, present attendees, meetings continue to be held throughout all organizations in record numbers with reckless abandon. Many people regard meetings as another waste of time; others see them as an unproductive way to pass the time. Some people have such great dislike for meetings that they feel stressed and anxious the moment they learn they have to attend one.

The typical meeting is called for by one person to convey information to many people. Ideally, the many reflect upon what they heard, come up with great ideas, and take bold, decisive action to the delight of the person who called for the meeting in the first place. As we all know, this rarely happens.

Instead, people shuffle into the meeting room, hear some new stuff that they have to do or learn or take back to others. Most of what they hear is quickly forgotten. Whatever they're supposed to do regarding the meeting is rarely done on time or in the fashion that the meeting manager had hoped for. There has to be a better way!

Elicit Encourage, attract, and make part of.

GET PEOPLE TO PARTICIPATE

A far more effective way to conduct a meeting is to elicit the participation of those who will be part of the meeting long before it starts. A
manager should take 2 to 4 minutes to speak with people who will be
attending the meeting in order to prepare them for what's going to
take place. At this time, the manager can hear their views about what
they're going to get out of the meeting and make them, in general,
partners as opposed to subjects.

For groups that have met on an ongoing basis, the meeting manager
could ask participants other types of questions, such as the following,
before the meeting:

- What's worked well for you in previous meetings?

- How can we proceed in a manner that involves everyone?

- What would you like to get out of this meeting?

This type of preparation may sound like extra work for the person
who's calling the meeting. Consider, however, that meetings aren't
held for the purposes of simply meeting; they're held (presumably) to
accomplish some worthwhile objective. If discussing with participants
how they can get the most from the forthcoming meeting will greatly
accelerate progress, why wouldn't a meeting manager want to do this?
After these discussions, the meeting itself is likely to take less time,
resulting in greater participation and, ideally, greater progress toward
the desired objective. That's real time management!

TIP

> Although some managers dread the thought of interviewing meeting participants before the meeting, participants are enthusiastic about this process. It makes them feel as though their input matters.

The act of interviewing attendees before the meeting also gives the meeting manager a leg up on exactly how to proceed:

1. He or she can design a custom agenda that focuses on topics identified as important to the entire group.

2. The agenda items can be arranged in a manner more conducive to the group's overall objectives.

3. When participants receive the agenda in advance, they come armed with an idea of how and when they can best contribute.

4. The meeting is far more likely to stay on course, end on time, and encourage participants to be more enthusiastic for the next meeting.

START THE MEETING ON TIME

When participants have a vested interest in the content of a meeting, they tend to arrive on time. When they receive an agenda in advance that lists the precise starting time, they have yet another indicator of the importance of being there. As the meeting manager, if you find people straggling in after the appointed start time, it behooves you to steadfastly start meetings on time so that people realize that they are late.

TIP

> Having everyone in the room acknowledge a tardy person by offering subtle looks can be a strong motivator for the tardy person to arrive on time afterward. Never discount the influence of peer pressure.

Robert Levasseur, in his book *Breakthrough Business Meetings,* suggests that at the start of any meeting, "participants reach a common understanding of what they're going to do and how they're going to do it." Levasseur says that this task normally consumes 10 percent of the meeting time, so if you're going to meet for 30 minutes, you need only 3 minutes or so to deal with the following basic issues:

- The main purpose of the meeting

- The participants' desired outcomes

- The sequence of agenda items

- The key meeting roles, which are understood at the outset in smaller groups

Use Hardball Incentives

If a few people still come to the meetings tardy after this new approach to meetings is in force, there are other techniques, with varying degrees of effectiveness, to encourage promptness:

- In my first job, if you were late for a meeting, you had to throw a dollar into the kitty for every minute you were late. Nobody ever walked in more than 5 minutes late. (I have no idea what the money was used for.)

- In some organizations, late-arriving people must apologize to the group. Then it becomes their responsibility afterwards to catch up with the group for the parts they missed; the meeting chair does not backtrack, which would cause everyone to wait while the tardy person received a personalized briefing.

- In one organization, the meeting room doors are locked when the meeting starts (not recommended!). Thereafter, if someone tries to get in, he or she has to knock on the door. Depending on how charitable the meeting manager is feeling, the knocks may be answered on the first round. The tardy person then sheepishly takes his or her seat.

CAUTION

In some organizations—and I do not condone this—tardy people are the subject of early discussion, gossip, innuendo, and outright jokes.

- In some organizations, plum assignments are handed out in the first few minutes of a meeting so that tardy people are left with the least desirable tasks. This system provides a great incentive for arriving early to meetings.

None of these techniques is as effective as interviewing participants and circulating an agenda before the meeting and demonstrating on a repeated basis that the meetings start promptly as scheduled.

Keep Meetings on Track

A strong agenda in the best possible sequence and with estimated time frames for each agenda item is the winning formula for having meetings stay on track. On occasion, discussion may ensue, and an item may end up requiring twice as much time as originally allotted. Often, however, participants make up for the coverage in one area by being even briefer in other areas.

TIP

When participants know in advance that a particular item is allotted, for example, 5 minutes, most people do their best to honor that time frame.

The meeting manager or group leader proceeds down the agenda, eliciting the input of task leaders as scheduled. Others are encouraged to participate after the task leader delivers his or her message. Each agenda item is discussed; participants keep in mind the following questions:

- What is the specific issue being discussed?

- What does the group want to accomplish in discussing the item?

- What action needs to be taken to handle the issue?

- Who will act?

- What resources does he or she require?

- When will the issue be resolved?

- When will the group discuss the results?

Upon successful conclusion of these questions, the group then moves onto the next issue.

Not all issues require proceeding through all these questions. Sometimes, an agenda item merely represents an announcement or a report to the group that doesn't require any feedback or any discussion. Sometimes, the issue at hand represents an executive briefing, because the matter has been resolved.

The following techniques are used by various organizations to keep meetings on track. Each technique has varying effectiveness depending on the purpose of your group, how often it meets, and your group's history:

- In groups where participants have been interviewed and an agenda has been circulated in advance, participants often time their remarks so that their comments will be completed within the allotted timeframes.

- Some groups keep a timer in plain view of all participants to encourage them to keep their comments brief. Others meet in a room with a wall clock in plain view.

- In some groups, the meeting manager announces who will be speaking next and how many minutes have been devoted to the topic on the agenda.

- In some groups, participants routinely circulate summaries of their comments, charts, or exhibits that illustrate the points they want to make. Then, they offer brief commentary and highlight what they have circulated.

PLAIN ENGLISH

Slack   Margin or extra room to accommodate anticipated potential shortfalls in planning.

When the meeting manager has assigned times to each issue, participants try to stay within those time frames. When the meeting manager has elicited time frames from the participants in advance, it behooves them to stay on track. After all, if you said you needed only 3 minutes, but you really needed 10 minutes, that represents poor planning.

A wise meeting manager knows the importance of building some slack into all meetings. For example, she or he may allocate 5 minutes for a topic that he or she will be covering personally, knowing that it will take only about 2 or 3 minutes. In this manner, several minutes can be saved here or there. Thus, if somebody goes over the allotted time frame, then the meeting still stays on track overall and ends on time or close to the time designated on the agenda.

Here are other ideas used to keep meetings on track:

- In some meetings, participants are asked to stand when they speak. This tends to limit the time that they speak, because most people would prefer to stay seated. Something about standing up and addressing a group strikes fear into the hearts of even the most seasoned professionals.

- Small group meetings of 18 people or fewer are usually held around several (connected or adjoined) tables put together or a circular table. Hence, if people stand and speak or speak from their seats instead of going to the front of the room, much time will be saved.

TIP

If someone can't come to the meeting, ask that person to submit what he or she would have said in a paragraph or two. You can then read this paragraph to the rest of the group.

- When meeting participants are encouraged to arrive early and are encouraged to stay afterwards, they are more likely to stick to business during the meeting. This is because they have time to banter and joke around both before and after the meeting, as opposed to attempting to do it during the meeting.

SET THE RIGHT ATMOSPHERE

The quickest way to lose the audience, other than being a boring speaker, is to speak in a room where the temperature is too high for participants or ventilation is poor. That, coupled with a dark meeting room, encourages people to fall asleep.

CAUTION

It's an anthropological phenomenon: As soon as it's dark, one's brain gets the message that it's okay to doze off. A warm room or a lack of oxygen aids the process.

You always want to meet in a well-lit room with excellent ventilation. If you have a choice between having a room be slightly too warm or slightly too cool, opt for cool. A cool room will keep participants fresh and alert. A cold room may prompt them to complain, but no one will doze off.

If participants need to take many notes or work from laptop computers, make sure there are flat surfaces on which they can work. Pens, pads, cold water, and possibly tea or coffee all can help.

If a meeting is going to last longer than 90 minutes, schedule breaks someplace in the middle for at least 5 to 8 minutes. You lose the attention of participants who are thinking about getting a tissue, making a phone call, or going to the bathroom. You also lose attention of participants because people's attention spans in this day and age are only so long.

Consider these room atmospherics when conducting a meeting:

- Meet in a room where participants won't be disturbed by ringing phones, people knocking on the door, and other intrusions.

- Meet in a room with wall-to-wall carpeting and walls adorned with pictures, posters, curtains, and the like to help absorb sounds and to offer a richer texture to the voices being heard. If you meet in a room with a tile floor, cold metal chairs, and blank, thin walls, participants will want the meeting to be over sooner, no matter what's being discussed.

- Meet in a room with comfortable seats that support the lumbar region of the back. Overly comfortable seats may encourage people to nod off.

TIP

Everyone's seat, ideally, should be the same. No one should be seated higher or lower than anyone else.

- If everyone already knows everyone else in the room, nametags are not necessary. In general, however, nametags or name cards on the table aid communication. When one can refer to the name of someone who just made a remark, the meeting takes on a warmer, friendlier tone, and participants have the opportunity to bond with each other more easily.

- In some groups, the secretary or transcriber takes notes of everything said. Other groups use a tape recorder, which is far more efficient, and have the notes transcribed afterwards. Either way, tape recorders, pocket dictaphones, overhead projectors, slides, chalkboards, whiteboards, and all other equipment should be set up far in advance and tested before the meeting begins. One should also check for replacement batteries, light bulbs, extension cords, and all supporting equipment.

ACHIEVE THE DESIRED OBJECTIVES

Some groups meet with an accountant, an attorney, or other advisor as a method of keeping the meeting on track or headed toward its desired objectives. Local chapter meetings of Toastmaster International, for example, include a parliamentarian who routinely advises the group members as to when they have strayed from established protocol.

Some groups choose to have one person serve as timer. The meeting manager or other designated professional also may choose to indicate when a matter is best handled by a subgroup such as a task force or select team to the group at hand. Former Secretary of State Dr. Henry Kissinger once said that there was no purpose in having a meeting unless the desired outcomes were known in advance. (He also said, "The absence of alternatives clears the mind marvelously.")

For those items on the agenda with a corresponding objective, the group leader or meeting manager has the responsibility to seek progress toward the objective. What else needs to be accomplished, and by when, to meet the overall objective? As you learned in Lesson 2, "Shaping Your Future," the overall objectives for those selected items need to be …

- written down.

- quantified.

- assigned specific time frames.

The meeting manager has the primary responsibility to maintain the atmosphere for all participants; otherwise, the meeting comes off as an edict: "I say; you do." Edicts don't encourage people to want to attend meetings in the future, nor be participants, even when something vital and interesting is presented.

PLAIN ENGLISH

Facilitator   The person charged with forwarding the action in regards to a particular event.

Most importantly, the meeting manager serves as facilitator, eliciting the best of responses from participants, encouraging them to cooperate with one another, and encouraging them to truly function as a team.

HANDLE RIFTS

In even the smallest of groups, the diverse backgrounds and personalities of participants ensure that there will be some clashes on occasion. A skilled meeting manager can help keep the disruption to a minimum.

Perhaps the rifts between individual participants can never truly be closed, but at least they can be minimized. For the good of the group and the accomplishment of its objectives, participants can be taught to understand that the whole needs to be larger than the sum of its parts. That can only be done through effective teamwork.

FOLLOW UP MEETINGS

The most effective meeting managers have the courage to engage in meeting follow-up. They meet with participants afterwards to find out what participants thought was effective in the meeting, what could be added, what could be dropped, and how meetings could be improved. The manager then ruminates on these suggestions and incorporates those that would make a significant contribution.

CAUTION

Too many managers, in the erroneous attempt to save time, don't bother to gather any feedback from participants following the meeting. They figure that their own observations were plenty, so why bother to take the time to consult with others?

If meeting participants are part of a team that is charged with meeting an objective, and the meeting manager can facilitate that by having more effective meetings, then listening to feedback from participants is ultimately a time-saver.

THE 30-SECOND RECAP

- Most meeting managers never bother to interview participants before a meeting to ensure an effective meeting. Yet if you want to achieve desired objectives, interviews represent a great time-saver.

- Circulating an agenda in advance with a list of topics and proposed time frames helps participants come to the meeting prepared and ready to stay on track.

- The meeting room atmospherics are as important as any other element of the meeting for ensuring that participants feel awake and alert. Hence, selection and inspection of the room beforehand and inspection of equipment and supporting items are crucial.

- Post-meeting interviews of participants to elicit their feedback and suggestions for meeting improvements can help to dramatically increase the effectiveness of future meetings.

LESSON 14
Managing Time on the Road

In this lesson, you will learn how to increase personal effectiveness by being productive while traveling by car, public transportation, or airplane.

BE PRODUCTIVE WHILE DRIVING

As each month passes, a variety of new electronic gadgets becomes available with increasing capabilities over those of their predecessors. Using plug-in or wireless equipment, you can connect with phones, faxes, e-mail accounts, the Web and everything in between. Regardless of the type of equipment you employ, the fundamentals of being productive while on the road stay relatively the same.

Make no mistake, when you're driving, your principal activity is driving. Studies show that driving while speaking on a cell phone quadruples the risk of an accident and increases the risk of dying in an accident 11 times. You can give your sharp attention in only one basic direction.

CAUTION

If you are pulled up to a traffic light or sitting in slow-moving traffic, it is still dangerous to talk on a cell phone, even a hands-free cell phone. Don't do it. Pull off to the side of the road if you must make a call.

Listening to music or speaking with someone in the passenger seat does not pose the same risk. The reason is that your sharp attention can continue to be on the road, and as practical, you can give some attention to the radio, CD, or the passenger in the seat next to you. However, at any given moment, your driving takes precedence. This is not the case with the use of the cell phone; concentrating on the conversation with someone at a distance and driving compete with one another.

If you ride with people on the way to work because you are part of a car pool or van pool, try to commute with those with whom you enjoy conversing. Surprisingly, you may have more lively conversations with someone who does not work with you and benefit from the cross-fertilization of ideas.

 TIP

> Keep your car windows closed and the heat or air conditioner on. Studies show that you will obtain the same miles per gallon as you do with the windows open and the heater or air conditioner off, and the ride will be much quieter.

If you decide to listen to something, play a CD or cassette that is invigorating or inspiring. Visit your library and find lectures, plays, and essays on cassettes or CDs. Or, play classical music whose rhythms and composition have been shown to promote healing and well-being as opposed to other forms of music, which can have a disconcerting effect.

MAKE THE MOST OF YOUR COMMUTE

A daily commute can be drudgery. You crawl along bumper to bumper, inhaling the fumes of the thousands of cars before you, on a superhighway that effectively operates like a slow-moving parking lot.

Whether the traffic is moving fast or slow, use commuting time to contemplate your day. Consider what is on your agenda for the morning, who you will be meeting, what you will be doing, and then see yourself successfully handling it all.

TIP

A major key to personal effectiveness while commuting is to use that time for reflection, instead of automatically flipping on the radio or engaging in some other activity that essentially represents filling the time.

One way to avoid the masses in the morning and afternoon is to depart when everyone else isn't. If you can leave an hour or an hour and a half earlier or later than everyone else, you're likely to have smoother sailing. Consider getting up at your normal time, working for an hour and a half at home, and then departing for the office. Perhaps you can do the same at the end of the day by leaving early in the afternoon, getting home without fighting a lot of traffic, and then working for another hour or hour and a half. Or perhaps you prefer to leave after everyone else does at the end of the day.

Once a week, try telecommuting instead of going into the office. These days almost everyone is wired to their offices by fax, modem, and telephone. If you can stay home even one Wednesday every other week, you'll find that you're far more productive in handling the kinds of tasks that are hard to tackle in a hectic office.

For variety, one time a week take a different route home. Even if you end up spending an extra 5 or 8 minutes driving home, it's worth it to see another section of town, to pass other stores and neighborhoods, and to stimulate your thinking.

CAUTION

> Commuting back and forth on exactly the same path day after day, week after week, can put you in a rut. Varying your routine a little can be beneficial in many ways.

PREPARE FOR CONTINGENCIES

Keeping your car in absolutely the best running condition is the first prerequisite to success on the road. You only have to break down once in a strange location to experience how unproductive a day can be. Take your car in for a tune-up on a regular basis, as the manufacturer recommends. It doesn't hurt to take the car in anytime you even suspect that something is not operating as it should be.

If you're not a member of one of the national auto clubs, it pays for you to become one. If you have to have your car jump-started or towed only once per year, the annual cost of membership has already paid for itself. Having this kind of security is priceless. By dialing an 800 number, you can have a top-flight garage with a qualified towing specialist on the scene almost wherever you are, usually in 45 minutes or less.

Keep an extra set of car keys someplace under the bumper in one of those hide-a-key compartments. Also, have spare house keys hidden in your car, just as you would have spare car keys somewhere in your house. Getting locked out is not productive. Having to call somebody to open your car is a waste of time and money.

Hide a roll of dimes and a roll of quarters in your car to use for parking meters, pay phones, and vending machines. Keep a back-up briefcase or folder in your trunk with stamps, envelopes, pen, paper, calculator, and perhaps important phone numbers. What else is worth storing in the car? A gym bag with socks, extra underwear, a toothbrush, tissues, flashlight, sunglasses, less frequently used credit cards, library cards, first aid kit, umbrella, a raincoat, a hat, and some gloves among other things.

If you ride with a notebook or palmtop computer, undoubtedly you have key addresses and key phone numbers with you. If not, hide important phone numbers, pin numbers, and access numbers some-place in your car where they will never be found, but where you can draw upon them in a hurry if you need to.

ORGANIZE YOUR ERRANDS

Instead of letting all your errands stack up for the weekends, designate one night per week as errand night. For example, make Monday, Tuesday, or Wednesday night the night when you handle errands on the way back from work. Prepare for multiple stops by making a brief list and affixing it to your dashboard.

Keep a file folder, envelope, or pouch handy for assembling the vari-ous tickets, sales slips, and so forth that you will be dispensing and collecting. If you can, keep the passenger side of your car clear so that it serves as your command center on wheels.

TIP

> Buy in bulk so you don't have to return to various stores as often, or have the stores come to you by finding vendors on the Internet who can pick up and deliver.

While running your errands, listen to books on tape or uplifting music as discussed previously. Whenever you control your environment, par-ticularly in your car, you have a better chance of staying energetic and alert. If you incur traffic backups, long lines, or other delays, fold up the tent and head home. It's no use trying to force your way through the crowds. You can handle errands another night, preserve your week-ends, and get it all done in less time and with less bother.

As more and more of what you need to do can be done via catalogs and the Internet, you may find that a couple of hours a week is more than enough to take care of errands. Rather than pick up stamps at the post office, order them by mail. Rather than dropping off deposits at the bank, mail them in. Every time that you don't have to get into your car to accomplish something, you save time, preserve your vehicle, and keep your sanity.

BE PRODUCTIVE ON PUBLIC TRANSPORTATION

If you are one of the less than 10 percent of the working population who gets to work via public transportation, my hat is off to you. Though cities have designed vast subway and bus systems, the majority of commuters still get to work by automobile. There are many ways to be productive while on a bus, subway, train, or van.

To tune out surrounding noise, use a portable cassette or CD player. Chose what you want to listen to, but make sure that it's uplifting, informative, and generally supports how you want to be and feel in life.

If you travel with a palmtop or notebook computer, you may wish to sit on the nonsunny side of the vehicle, depending on the brightness of your screen. Also, be sure to have plenty of recharged batteries available for the ride. Murphy's Law says that your batteries will fail you about 5 minutes after you get started. Quash that possibility by always traveling with fresh batteries, and having a backup pair ready to draw upon.

PLAIN ENGLISH

Murphy's Law   The age-old axiom stating that if something can go wrong, it will go wrong.

CAUTION

> Do not house your expensive computer in a traditional carrying case, because these are targets for thieves. Instead, carry expensive equipment in a satchel or worn briefcase.

The lighter that you travel, the more adept you will be at getting on and off the bus, subway, train, or other vehicle. If you have been commuting for any length of time, you know how long the ride will take, so you can plan your work accordingly. I've seen many adept professionals practice what I call vest-pocket management. They are able to pull out a pad or pen, business cards, Post-It notes, a palmtop computer, a handheld calendar, a pocket dictator, or variety of other work-related tools from their vest pocket, get to work at the drop of a hat, and pack up just as quickly. If you continually have to fumble through a large briefcase to find a pen or key folder, you're not going to be highly efficient while working on public transportation.

If you read a lot during your time on public transportation, bring materials you can quickly pare down. For example, if you are plowing through several magazines, quickly detach the articles that appear to be of interest and recycle the rest of the magazine. You may want to purchase a small *slasher* (available in any office supply store), which enables you to deftly remove articles from a newspaper or magazine by making a light incision around what you have selected. Your goal while traveling is to always have less at the end of your trip to carry.

TIP

> Always retain the smallest volume of paper that serves your purposes. For example, save the one page from an article that contains key information instead of saving the whole thing.

With the availability of hand-held scanners, you can now travel with a pocket scanner, scan in one line of a document at a time, and end up carrying little paper. Likewise, if you travel with a pocket dictator, simply dictate the key phrases, phone numbers, and other tidbits of information you want to retain. Later you can transcribe your own tape or have someone else transcribe it and have the information on hard disk.

If you travel with a cell phone, be respectful of other passengers. Turn away from the open area, modulate your voice, and keep your conversations as short as practical. You may think that you're taking care of all kinds of business and that you're so efficient, but to everyone else around you, you are a crashing bore.

Checking for voice mail messages, e-mail, and other correspondence can now, of course, all be easily handled while in transit. However, don't whip yourself into a frenzy over the gathering of these messages. They will all still be there when you arrive at your destination. Too many career professionals, in the erroneous belief that they have to stay connected, wired, and available every nanosecond of the day, heap far more stress and anxiety upon themselves than the previous generation of career professionals ever had to contend with.

CAUTION

Incessantly checking voice mail and e-mail is usually not the hallmark of a highly efficient person; it's the hallmark of someone who is obsessed.

FLY THE FRIENDLY SKIES

With increasing passenger loads and more restrictive airline configurations, airline travel has become increasingly stressful in the last few years. The key to being productive while traveling by air is to stay light and take care of as many things as you can beforehand:

- Pack the night before and pack as light as you can.

- Use the smallest possible size of various toiletries.

- Use rolling luggage so that you don't have to lift your bag. Most airlines will accept carry-on luggage of 22 inches by 14 inches by 9 inches. Thus, you can roll your luggage onto the plane and never have to check your bag, which saves a good 15 to 20 minutes at the end of each flight.

- Don't pack anything that you know your hotel or host destination already supplies. You can always call in advance to get the list of what is offered. You'll have a lot more room in your suitcase if you don't have to pack a bathrobe, an alarm clock, a hairdryer, and so on.

The airlines will let you take two bags on board. If you have to pack a second bag, use something that fits on the top of your rolling cart luggage so that you can roll them both instead of lifting either bag. If the second bag is your briefcase, pack it lightly and efficiently. If you have to have more than two bags, you might as well check them all, because waiting for one bag is roughly going to be equal to the time you have to wait for all of your bags.

If you have a lengthy trip with many stops, rather than bringing enough clothes for each day, bring enough clothing for half the trip plus one day. In other words, if you are traveling for 9 days, bring 5 days' worth of clothing. If you are traveling for 10 days, bring 6 days' worth of clothing. Then, as you approach half of your trip, get everything cleaned while on the road. Taking advantage of laundry and valet services costs a little money, but you're far better off dispensing a few dollars here and there than toting an incredible burden of heavy clothing.

Bring U.S. Priority Mail packages with you so that as you collect paper information during your travels you can mail them back to yourself rather than continuing to carry them. At a little more than $3, a U.S. Priority Mail pack is relatively inexpensive, is made of tyvek material so that it can't rip, and has a self-adhesive closing flap. You can stuff the package full, and the post office hardly ever loses them. Bring address labels for both your destination and your home base to save you from having to write out your name and address.

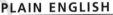

PLAIN ENGLISH

Valet   Traditionally, a personal attendant; hotel/ business services that pick up and drop off of gar- ments and other personal items.

Book Your Flight and Get It Right

Never, ever buy tickets at the airline counters the day of your depar- ture. If you do, you're likely to get the worst seats at the highest price. You want to buy your tickets in advance so that you can get the bulk- head, the wing row, or an aisle, each of which offer more room than being in the middle or in a window location. If you prefer the window, fine. Most business travelers want the flexibility of an aisle seat. On an aisle seat, you can get to the bathroom more easily, you can stretch, and you can get to the magazine rack if you so choose.

Always bring a water bottle with you so that you don't have to wait for flight attendants to come around to quench your thirst. A few sips here and there can make all the difference between maintaining high energy and high productivity, and being sluggish, dehydrated, and not getting the quality of work done that you had hoped to. Always bring your own snacks. Pack carrots, cucumbers, apples, bananas, sunflower seeds, peanuts, and anything else that is healthful and will give you an energy boost.

CAUTION

Avoid bringing heavily sugared or salted snacks that offer nothing more than empty carbohydrates. These snacks will drain you of energy, leave your body starved for nutrients, and make you far less efficient.

If you're meeting a client after you touch down, you may have to wear your full business suit; otherwise, wear loose and comfortable clothing. You want to be able to move around freely. Sitting in an airplane seat for hours can be confining. Of late, with smaller seats and heavier passengers, it can be an ordeal. Avoid heavy clothing, tight shoes, restrictive belts, and anything else that reduces respiration, ventilation, and circulation.

If you're flying in the middle of the day and the sun's ultraviolet rays are more pronounced, especially if you're flying above the clouds, don some sunglasses. Also use the airline overhead lighting and lower your window cover. Your eyes won't get nearly as fatigued.

 TIP

> If you need to sleep on the plane, put on a baseball cap with a message on the rim saying something like "Sleeping, do not disturb." If you need to work, consider wearing a cap that says, "On deadline, please do not disturb." You'd be surprised how well people obey these messages.

Avoid alcohol anytime during your flight, even if it's at the end of the day, you are heading home, and there is no more work to be done. You might think that it is relaxing to finish off the day with a beer, wine, or other alcoholic beverage, but you'll end up dehydrated and more tired than you would otherwise feel. If you need a nightcap, wait until you are home.

THE 30-SECOND RECAP

- In a highly mobile society, the chances are increasing that you will be spending some time in a moving vehicle. By making adequate preparations beforehand, you maximize your potential for being at your best while in motion and afterwards.

- Assemble in advance the equipment, reporting items, snack items, and other creature comforts that enhance the way you work and rest. This will give you the highest probability of being productive while on the road.

- Check for voice and e-mail messages periodically throughout the day, but don't become obsessed about it. You don't need to check every few minutes.

Glossary

backup system   An established procedure whereby you help to reinforce established goals.

being organized   Arranging one's possessions, time, or life, so as to remain comfortably in control.

bots   Software enabling you to automatically extract and receive information gathered from the Web based on your parameters or specifications.

cellular intelligence   The ability of the body down to the cellular level to respond to stimulus in the immediate environment.

clutter   An unorganized accumulation of items, the collective value of which is suspect.

date stamping   The process of fixing a date to items as they arrive, and preferably before they are filed.

elicit   Encourage, attract, and make part of.

environment   One's surroundings; in the context of the workaday world, one's office and surrounding offices and, in general, one's work place.

ergonomics   The relationship between furniture, equipment, resources, and individuals engaged in using them.

facilitator   The person charged with forwarding the action in regards to a particular event.

Gantt chart   A linear, visual tool for measuring progress made in pursuit of various activities over the course of time.

mettle   Value or worthiness, particularly when tested by challenging conditions.

Murphy's Law   The age-old axiom stating that if something can go wrong, it will go wrong.

Pareto's Principle   An observation about the relationship between inputs and outputs, essentially that 80 percent of one's effectiveness is derived from 20 percent of one's activities.

Personal Digital Assistants (PDA)   Another name for handheld computing devices or palmtops.

physiology   The science that deals with processes and functions of living organisms.

prereader   Someone who serves as an information scout for another, paring down voluminous reading materials to their essence.

priority list   A simple roster, preferably easy to access, that names a handful of things in life important to you.

quiet time   An interval during the day in which you are not subjected to noise.

reinforcement   Reward directly following a particular behavior.

scheduling tools   Palmtop organizers, electronic calendars, time management software, day planners, and any other device that supports one's use of time and productivity.

slack   Margin or extra room to accommodate anticipated potential short falls in planning.

time and motion studies   The attempt to elicit greater productivity from workers by closely examining their workstations, movements, and available resources.

urgent   That which cries out for attention independent of its importance, typically announcing itself much like a microwave beeping when it's time to take the food out of it.

valet   Traditionally, a personal attendant; hotel/business services that pick up and drop off garments and other personal items.

volunteering   Willingly giving of one's time or effort.

white noise   Frequencies and amplitudes of a droning, non-disruptive blanket of sound.

your life's priorities   That which is most important to you.

Further Reading

Blanke, Gail. *In My Wildest Dreams: Living the Life You Long For.* New York: Simon & Schuster, 1998.

Bykofsky, Sheree. *500 Terrific Ideas for Organizing Everything.* New York: Budget Book Service, 1997.

Cathcart, Jim. *Acorn Principle.* New York: St. Martins Press, 1998.

Davidson, Jeff. *Breathing Space: Living & Working at a Comfortable Pace in a Sped-up Society.* New York: Mastermedia, 2000.

_____. *Joy of Simple Living.* Emmaus, PA: Rodale Books, 1999.

_____. *Market Your Career and Yourself.* Holbook, MA: Adams Media, 1999.

_____. *Complete Idiot's Guide to Managing Stress.* New York: Macmillan, 1999.

_____. *Complete Idiot's Guide to Managing Your Time.* New York: Macmillan, 1999.

_____. *Complete Idiot's Guide to Reaching Your Goals.* New York: Macmillan, 1998.

Dawson Roger. *13 Secrets of Power Performance.* Paramus, NJ: Prentice Hall, 1994.

Felton, Sandra. *Messie's Manual.* Grand Rapids, MI: Fleming A. Drevel, 1983.

Fritz, Robert. *Path of Least Resistance.* New York: Ballantine Books, 1989.

Hobbs, Charles. *Time Power.* New York: Harper & Row, 1987.

Kimeldorf, Martin. *Serious Play, A Leisure Wellness Guidebook.* Berkeley: Ten Speed, 1994.

Koch, Richard. *The 80/20 Principle: The Secret to Success by Achieving More With Less.* New York: Doubleday, 1999.

Lakein, Andrew. *How To Get Control of Your Time and Your Life.* New York: Wyden Books, 1973.

Levasseur, Robert. *Breakthrough Business Meetings.* Holbrook, MA: Adams Media, 1994.

McCay, James. *Management of Time.* Paramus, NJ: Prentice Hall, 1959.

Moskowitz, Robert. *How to Organize Your Work and Your Life.* San Diego: Mainstream Books, 1981.

Salsbury, Glenna. *Art of the Fresh Start.* Deerfield Beach, FL: Health Communications, 1995.

Shank, David. *Data Smog.* New York: HarperCollins, 1997.

Sharma, Robert S. *Monk Who Sold His Ferrari.* San Francisco: HarperCollins, 1998.

Wieder, Marsha. *Doing Less Having More.* New York: Morrow, 1998.

INDEX

Jeff Davidson is frequently called to speak at conferences, conventions, and retreats. He has made presentations to 580 groups in North America, Europe, and Asia on topics related to staying productive and competitive, yet remaining balanced and happy while confronting constant change. Comments such as "Best of the Convention," or "Best we've ever heard," represent typical feedback to Jeff's presentations.

Jeff is the author of numerous books, thousands of articles, and nine audio and video programs. Jeff's six-cassette album, *Simplifying Your Work and Your Life* (SkillPath), which he corecorded with Dr. Tony Alessandra, gives career professionals the tools and practical information they need to address the complexity in their everyday lives.

Jeff offers a blend of keynote and seminar presentations on how to maintain balance while remaining profitable and competitive. His presentations include

- Relaxing at High Speed™
- Managing Multiple Priorities
- Overworked or Overwhelmed?™
- Handling Information and Communication Overload

In recent years, several of Jeff's speeches (including "Relaxing at High Speed," "Choosing when it's Confusing," "Overworked or Overwhelmed?" "World Population and Your Life," and "Handling Information Overload") have been published in issues of the prestigious *Vital Speeches of the Day,* alongside those of Dr. Henry Kissinger, Lee Iacocca, William Bennett, Michael Eisner, and Alan Greenspan.

The Washington Post, where he's been featured eight times, called Jeff Davidson a "dynamo of business book writing." Millions of people have read about Jeff in *USA Today,* the *Los Angeles Times,* the *San Francisco Chronicle,* and the *Chicago Tribune,* or have seen him featured on *Good Morning America, CBS Nightwatch,* CNBC, *Ask Washington,* and hundreds of regionally based talk shows.

To obtain a comprehensive list of resources, including additional information on Jeff's keynote and breakout presentations and Jeff's speech availability, visit the Breathing Space Institute's Web site at www.BreathingSpace.com, fax to 919-932-9982, e-mail jeff@BreathingSpace.com, or call Jeff directly at 919-932-1996.